STUDIO
CERAMICS

PETER LANE

Chilton Book Company
Radnor, Pennsylvania

Published in Radnor,
Pennsylvania 19089 in 1983
by Chilton Book Company

Copyright © Peter Lane 1983

Art Editor: Janet James
Designer: Caroline Hill
Editor: Cathy Gosling

Library of Congress
Catalog Card No. 83–70247
ISBN 0-8019-7306-6

Printed and bound in
Hong Kong by South China Printing Co.

Front jacket: James Tower
Title page: Dorothy Feibleman
Back jacket:
Robin Welch (above left)
Gotlind Weigel (above right)
Paula Winokur (below left)
Martin Smith (below right)

CONTENTS

POTTERS FEATURED

AUSTRALIA
Christine Ball
Joan Campbell
Greg Daly
John Dermer
Lorraine Lee
Janet Mansfield
Vincent McGrath
Anne Mercer
Jeff Mincham
Bruce Nuske
Diane Peach
Alan Peascod
Gwyn Pigott
Derek Smith
Ian Sprague
Hiroe Swen
Josef Szirer
Sandra Taylor
John Teschendorff
Bryan Trueman
Alan Watt

CANADA
Keith Campbell
John Chalke
Diane Creber
Neil Dalrymple
Walter Dexter
Monique Ferron
Franklyn Heisler
Robin Hopper
Harlan House
Yvette Mintzberg
Ann Mortimer
Wayne Ngan
Maurice Savoie
David Toresdahl

EUROPE

AUSTRIA
Kurt Spurey

BELGIUM
Antoine Richard Crül
Carmen Dionyse
Antoine de Vinck

DENMARK
Alev Siesbye

FRANCE
Pierre Bayle
Claude Champy

WEST GERMANY
Heinar Balzar
Antje Bruggemann-
Breckwoldt
Dieter Crumbiegel
Volker Ellwanger
Christa Gebhardt
Johannes Gebhardt
Beate Kuhn
Karl Scheid
Ursula Scheid
Margarete Schott
Hildegard Storr-Britz
Fritz Vehring
Vera Vehring
Gerald Weigel
Gotlind Weigel

HOLLAND
Marianna Franken
Vilma Henkelman
Hans de Jong
Michel Kuipers
Jan Van Leeuwen
Johan Van Loon
Johnny Rolf
Jan de Rooden

HUNGARY
Imre Schrammel

ITALY
Nino Caruso

NORWAY
Dagny Hald
Finn Hald
Ingvil Havrevold
Erik Pløen

POLAND
Maria Kuczynska
Anna Zamorska

SWEDEN
Stig Lindberg
Ulla Viotti

UK
Godfrey Arnison
Oldrich Asenbryl
Gordon Baldwin
Alan Barratt-Danes
Ruth Barratt-Danes
Val Barry
Glenys Barton
Michael Bayley
Peter Beard
Tony Bennett
Maggie Berkowitz
Sebastian Blackie
Alison Britton
Hilary Brock
Graham Burr
Alan Caiger-Smith
Michael Casson
Sheila Casson
John Chipperfield
Gordon Cooke
Delan Cookson
Emmanuel Cooper
Hans Coper
Jill Crowley
Geoffrey Eastop
David Eeles
Siddig El'Nigoumi
Dorothy Feibleman
Vivienne Foley
Robert Fournier
Sheila Fournier
Ruth Franklin
Elizabeth Fritsch
Tessa Fuchs
Marian Gaunce
Jane Hamlyn
Henry Hammond
Alan Heaps
Ewen Henderson

Karin Hessenberg
Nicholas Homoky
Glyn Hugo
Walter Keeler
Peter Lane
David Leach
Eileen Lewenstein
Mal Magson
Jim Malone
West Marshall
Eric James Mellon
Bryan Newman
Eileen Nisbet
John Pollex
Jacqueline Poncelet
Lucie Rie
Mary Rogers
Peter Simpson
Martin Smith
Gillian Still
Geoffrey Swindell
Janice Tchalenko
James Tower
Angela Verdon
Jenny Welch
Robin Welch
Mary White
Alan Whittaker
Gary Wornell
Rosemary Wren
and Peter Crotty

NEW ZEALAND
Rosemarie Brittain
David Brokenshire
Len Castle
Roy Cowan
Ian Firth
Leo King
Jack Laird
John Parker
Debbie Pointon
Rick Rudd
Mirek Smíšek
Peter Stichbury

USA

Rudy Autio
Curtis Benzle
Susan Benzle
Mona Brooks
Virginia Cartwright
Philip Cornelius
Glenn Doell

Ruth Duckworth
Nina Gaby
Harvey Goldman
Erik Gronborg
Dorothy Hafner
Catherine Hiersoux
Sylvia Hyman
Karen Karnes

Gudrun Klix
Henry Lyman
Scott Malcolm
Tim Mather
Otto Natzler
Sally Bowen Prange
Eileen Richardson
James Rothrock

Jill Ruhlman
Kaete Brittin Shaw
Paul Soldner
John Takehara
Tom Turner
Paula Winokur
Robert Winokur

ACKNOWLEDGEMENTS

I would like to record my thanks to all the potters in the book who have generously contributed information and photographs of their work, including details of their personal motivation and their individual techniques.

Once again, I am indebted to my editor Cathy Gosling, who worked with me on my previous book *Studio Porcelain* and has continued to give me patient guidance, faith and constant encouragement. I am also grateful to the designers, Janet James and Caroline Hill, who have dealt very imaginatively with the immensely complicated task of integrating so many illustrations with the text.

I would also like to thank the following photographers, organizations, museums and individuals who have kindly granted permission for their photographs to be reproduced:

John Anderson, p. 181 (above); p. 194 (right); Paul Anthony, p. 169 (left); Neil Badger, p. 130 (right); Hugo Barclay, p. 160 (below); Robert E. Barrett, p. 83; Jean-Pierre Beaudin, p. 15 (below); p. 152 (above); Robyn Beeche, p. 61 (above and below); Margareta Berquist, p. 10 (above); John Billar, p. 48 (below); Hedrich Blessing, p. 149 (below); Lillian Bolvinkel, p. 43; Yvan Boulerice, p. 9; Brian Brake, p. 198 (right); Jon Brooks, p. 60 (below left); Volker Bruggemann, p. 175 (below); Graham Burr, p. 159 (below); Albert Clitheroe, p. 21 (below right); p. 41; The Crafts Council, p. 23 (above); p. 23 (below right) (photograph by Council of Industrial Design (CoID)); p. 26 (above); p. 26 (below) (photograph by CoID); p. 38 (left and right); p. 39 (photograph by CoID); p. 75 (photograph by Mike Freeman); p. 98 (below); p. 99 (above); p. 102 (below) (photograph by Mike Freeman); p. 204 (above) (photograph by David Ward); p. 204 (below) (photograph by Mike Freeman); p. 205 (above) (photograph by Mike Freeman); p. 214 (below) (photograph by CoID); Tadeusz Chmielowiec, p. 187 (below left and right); David Cripps, p. 162 (above); p. 247; Madeline Dinkel, p. 194 (below); Larry Dixon, p. 147 (below right); p. 179; p. 180 (above and below); p. 192; Ian Dobbie, p. 240; G. Doren, p. 42 (right); H. Elofsson, p. 137; M. Lee Fatherree, p. 191 (below right); Joseph Felzman, p. 18 (left); p. 167 (above and below); Foto-Studio Baumann, p. 198 (above); Courtney Frisse, p. 8; p. 119 (below); John Fuller, p. 138 (below right); C. Gallet, p. 117 (above); Bernd Peter Göbbels, p. 28 (above); p. 108; Jack Goodchild, p. 84; p. 154 (above); Cliff Guttridge, p. 23 (above); p. 163 (above and below); p. 244 (below);

Hadler/Rodriguez, p. 213 (below); Grant Hancock, p. 8 (left); p. 226 (above); p. 227; Bob Hanson, p. 93 (below); Tim Hill, p. 281 (below); Howard Huff, p. 191 (above); p. 217 (above right); Ben Johnson, p. 71; p. 210; G. Kalden, p. 136 (left); Michael Kluranek, p. 77 (above); Anthony Koscumb, p. 96 (above); Harold Lackner, p. 56 (below); Tony Latham, p. 118; Leeds Art Galleries, p. 105 (photograph by Ron Collier); Lelkes, p. 14; Kathy and Mark Lindquist, p. 60 (above and below right); D.J. Lindsey, p. 47 (above); John McKay, p. 131; Peter Macomber, p. 97 (above); Trey Mainwaring III, p. 198 (left); Michael Manni, p. 181 (above right) (loaned by kind permission of Henry Rothschild); Per Maurtvedt, p. 148 (above and below); p. 198 (above); Eric James Mellon, p. 211 (below); Eric Mitchell, p. 66, p. 245; Museum of Decorative Art, Copenhagen, p. 30 (above); Katherine Nathan, p. 143 (left); Alan Nisbet, p. 13 (below); p. 112 (above and below); Karen Norquay, p. 119 (above); p. 231 (below); Bill Parish, p. 19, p. 102 (above); Bernd Perlbach, p. 7; p. 134; p. 172 (right); L. de Rammelaere, p. 54; p. 120 (above); p. 121 (above); Gail Reynolds-Natzler, p. 25 (below); p. 40 (right); p. 87 (above); Rodriguez, Stuttgart, p. 88 (above); Richard Sargent, p. 29; Jochen Schade, p. 6; p. 28 (above and right); p. 88 (below); p. 109 (above and below); p. 143 (below); p. 159 (above); p. 166 (right); p. 178 (above); p. 197; Peter Schoonen, p. 128; p. 129 (above); p. 138 (below left); p. 186 (above); p. 187 (above); Roger Schreiber, p. 27; Scianamblo/Benzle, p. 135; p. 183 (above and below); Robert G. Smith, p. 173 (above); Christian M. Springer, p. 56 (above); Philip Starrett, p. 94; p. 95 (above and below); p. 170 (above); James Storr, p. 198 (below); Studio Roels Freddy, p. 55 (above); Studio 12, Waikanae, p. 229 (above and below); Studio 70, Langport, p. 12 (above); p. 146 (above and below); Studio 80, Grasberg, p. 87 (below); Teigensfoto Atelier A/S, p. 111; p. 133 (below); p. 172 (left); Monika Thein, p. 116; Les Thomas, p. 171 (right); p. 201 (above); p. 207 (above); Douglas Thompson, p. 233 (above); R.E. Tigges, p. 106 (centre); Stephanie Vail, p. 12 (below); p. 218 (above); p. 219 (above and below); Bart Vansteelant, p. 139; p. 140; Hans Vos, p. 117 (below); David Ward, p. 242; Cor van Weele, p. 36; p. 181 (middle right and below right); p. 196 (above); West Surrey College of Art and Design, p. 20 (above right); Ian Yeomans, p. 72 (above).

PREFACE

The field of studio ceramics has undergone considerable expansion since the early 1950s stimulated by much invention, ingenuity and enthusiasm throughout the world. It is an area in which creativity is bounded only by the technical knowledge and expertise of the potter. Even the so-called limitations of the ceramic medium are being increasingly overcome as more and more people take up its challenge. A veritable explosion of ideas has blown aside some recognized conventions and much taboo while stimulating new approaches to familiar problems of design and manufacture.

This exciting freshness and vitality is a truly international phenomenon, although evidence of the historical, social and cultural background sometimes remains to distinguish the work of one country from that of another. The enormous range of ceramic imagery is constantly growing. Visual statements realized through clay can exist as meaningful objects to delight, amuse, or provoke thought. Ceramic forms, whether large or small in scale, be they decorative, functional or sculptural, are the products of mental and physical application in response to human sensibility or need. As such, expression is infinite. In this context it is interesting to compare the various ways in which individual potters working in different situations have used similar specialised techniques or processes while adapting them to suit particular requirements. I do not presume to dictate taste or to pontificate about the relative merits of the works illustrated in this book but invite the reader to exercise his or her own critical faculties if and when aesthetic judgement may be necessary. My intention, rather, is to present a rich and varied selection of visual material, representative (as far as time and space allows) of some of the many approaches to the use of ceramic materials currently employed by a variety of craftsmen

'Figurine'. Slab-built porcelain with wire-cut relief pattern and black metallic glaze. Height $6\frac{5}{16}$in(16cm). Fired in oxidation to 1300°C. By CHRISTA GEBHARDT (West Germany), 1982.

OPPOSITE: 'Ringtower'. Red stoneware body, two layers of different glazes for both colours; the glaze with spots contains a local slip. Height $10\frac{1}{2}$in(26cm). The piece is constructed from thrown elements joined together. Electric kiln fired to cone 6a. By BEATE KUHN (West Germany), 1979.

in the Western world. I hope that in considering these forms and images together with the methods used in their creation, readers will be stimulated into greater awareness and appreciation of both the problems of the medium and of its potential for expression.

The starting-point for work in ceramics may lie within the actual techniques or materials, it may be developed in response to specific experience, or it may arise while grappling with elements of design or even through some spontaneous action. Possibly due to my role as a teacher of ceramics, I have always been intrigued to discover the motivation, thought processes and technology behind the artefact. Therefore, I have concentrated upon these aspects to describe in detail some of the many ways in which individual potters work.

Although the influence of oriental ceramics and philosophy, particularly that of China, Korea and Japan, remains strong among potters producing mainly functional domestic wares, the major part of this book

LEFT: Raku vase, wheel-thrown in two sections and joined, brushed white slip, sgraffito drawing at leather-hard stage, copper oxide wash and sprayed clear glaze, fired to 1060°C. Height 23⅝in(60cm). By JEFF MINCHAM (Australia), 1982.

'I am no longer that which I have been'. Stoneware slab construction, slips and residual salt firing to cone 3. 23 × 10 × 29in (58.4 × 25.4 × 73.7cm). By ANN MORTIMER (Canada), 1981.

is concerned with the work of those potters who have extended or broken established traditions. It is, perhaps, inevitable that the production of utilitarian wares offers less scope for genuine innovation. That is not to deny that interesting new ideas in table-wares continue to be developed alongside satisfying, highly competent, yet traditional vessel forms with which we are more familiar. Accordingly, the majority of works illustrated here are pieces that have come into existence as a result of the exploration of idea, material and form without concern for 'usefulness'.

I am acutely aware that my conscious decision to exclude work from Japan and from a number of other important countries, notably in Europe, may disappoint some readers, but the line had to be drawn somewhere and I chose to confine my researches mainly to British, North American and Australasian potters whom I knew or could contact. Similarly, from an historical point of view, it might be argued that there are several well-known and respected potters who have been omitted. However, my intention is to present a wide range of forms and imagery supported by working methods, rather than to produce a chronological treatise on twentieth-century studio pottery; although innovations, • developments and influences are mentioned where appropriate.

Each of the potters has evolved an individual style and feeling for ceramics. All would agree that no one way of working out ideas through the medium is necessarily more 'right' than another, just 'different'. They readily acknowledge influences of many kinds and these may or may not be observed in the finished piece. Not all the work shown will meet with universal approval but the spectator makes what must be, ultimately, a subjective judgement such as might be applied to the assessment of other areas of human expression.

Some of the potters included in this book prefer to be regarded as 'sculptors' or 'artists' because they feel that the terms 'craftsman' and 'potter' have limited horizons. They see their work as falling within the (artificial?) category of 'fine art'. The latter, as generally interpreted, seems to imply a superior plane of human activity. Ceramics, probably due to its domestic associations, suffers more than any other medium through this conflict of definitions. Yet, as the art historian and critic, Herbert Read, pointed out, a simple pot can be the purest

'Bal de Têtes'. Bottle, coil-built, fibreglass, raku glazes and oxides, cone 08 followed by post-firing reduction and smoking. Height $11\frac{7}{16}$in(29cm). By MONIQUE FERRON (Canada), 1982.

BELOW: 'Portnoy's Complaint No. 1'. Stoneware and glass, assembled from thrown sections, oxidised wood-ash glaze. Height 13in(33cm). By DELAN COOKSON (UK), 1981.

Bowl, white stoneware, modelled 'human figures' pressed into plaster mould and rolled together with a plaster ball. Diameter $17\frac{7}{16}$in(45cm). Cobalt oxide wash, rubbed off top surface with steel wool. Fired in oxidation. By ULLA VIOTTI (Sweden), 1980.

Bowl, stoneware, press-moulded slab construction, with iron oxide rubbed in. Diameter 20in(50.8cm). By YVETTE MINTZBERG (Canada).

form of abstract expression. A kind of absolute art? Why is it then that 'pottery' suffers from such inferior status? Processes of thought, feeling, content and intended purpose leading to a work should matter more than any ill-conceived labels supporting rigid assumptions.

Meanings associated with words like 'artist' and 'craftsman' are rooted in history but their relationship has shifted and become distorted by abuse. The 'craftsman' is respected for being highly skilled with his hands while it is usually the 'artist' from whom innovation, stimulation and, perhaps, controversy is expected. By such an interpretation, ideas and the expression of emotions appear to be the sole preserve of the 'artist'. It is, therefore, understandable that those clayworkers who wish to declare their intentions and work as being orientated towards the 'fine art' end of the spectrum should refer to themselves as 'ceramist' or 'ceramic sculptor'. If their work were executed in metal or stone or plastics or wood, the physical scale of individual pieces would help towards identifying non-

functional objects, whether good or bad, as something to do with 'fine' as opposed to 'applied' or 'decorative' art. In one sense, pottery still carries a stigma associated with expendability. It is easily broken, thrown away and replaced. Yet pottery (ceramics) mirrors the society which made it. That which has survived the centuries gives archaeology its greatest clues to civilisations long vanished. Pots made in a peasant society hundreds of years ago still possess the power to stir emotions: the prerequisite of all works of art. Again the label really

does not matter. Words are inadequate and superfluous before the object. This communication is visual, tactile and emotional above all else. As John Berger says, "seeing comes before words. The child looks and recognizes before it can speak."

Most people would define 'craft' as a refined form of manual activity; skill in the co-ordination of hand, eye and brain. My dictionary defines 'art' as "skill, especially human skill applied to imitation and design as in painting etc.; thing in which skill may be exercised". However, 'craft' also is de-

'Racing Car'. Stoneware with stained slips and barium glaze over a yellow matt glaze, fired to 1260°C in oxidation. Length 8in(23cm). The head is connected to the rear wheels by rods and an eccentric cam. This causes the head to move from side to side when the car is pushed along. By ALAN HEAPS (UK), 1981.

Teapot, jug, lidded jar and plate, porcelain decorated with coloured slips. By DOROTHY HAFNER (USA).

'Noah at Rest'. Stoneware. Height $7\frac{7}{8}$in(20cm). Boat shape made by lining a half ball mould with coils and then pushing this into the form of a boat. Deck coils added, and coils to represent timber planking. 'Stones' made from solid clay. Fired in neutral atmosphere to cone 9. By DIANE PEACH (Australia), 1981.

fined as skill, in fact "skill; art . . ." While, on the same page, 'crafty' is defined as "artful"! I then discover that 'artefact' is given as "a product of human art and workmanship". It would appear, therefore, that 'art' and 'craft' cannot really be separated and differences in status or appreciation arise from misconceptions concerning the actual materials used in the work. It might also be argued that, until the twentieth century, even artists had to be good craftsmen!

The dictionary definition of potter is "a maker of earthenware vessels"; and for pottery, "earthenware, potter's work". Note the emphasis on the manual and functional aspects to the exclusion of any hint of individual expression. 'Ceramics', on the other hand, is generally accepted to be an all-embracing term which even my dictionary confirms as "the art of pottery".

The popular interpretation of craft is likely to remain primarily concerned with the fashioning of objects intended to perform some domestic function. Similarly, the traditional view of the potter is of one who mainly makes hollow vessels for the storage

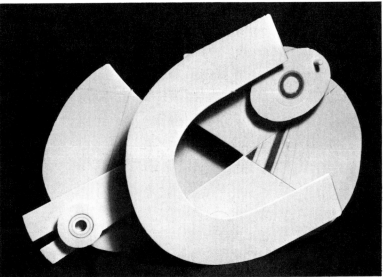

'Oval Abstract'. Slab construction in porcelain, inlaid and painted with coloured slips. $10\frac{5}{8} \times 7\frac{1}{16} \times 2\frac{3}{4}in(27 \times 18 \times 7$cm). Assembled after firing in electric kiln to 1240°C. By EILEEN NISBET (UK), 1981.

of food, liquids and so on, irrespective of the fact that, throughout history, potters have exercised intellect, skill, sensitivity and ingenuity in controlling earth, water and fire to provide an enormous range of powerful imagery (not necessarily vessel forms) for social, cultural or religious purposes.

Whatever labels are used, the fact remains that clay is a very special material to which we respond in our different ways. Through the ceramic processes we can explore ideas, impulses and feelings as pure form (possibly allied to some practical function), or as descriptive personal comment upon things observed, or as genuine abstract expression. The same holds true of any other material used in the production of art or craft. The point of my argument is that the material *itself* is irrelevant in deciding classification. I believe that any attempt to categorise individual objects as 'art' or 'craft' is an unnecessary and pointless exercise. The product of a sensitive mind and skilled hands must stand in its own right as a form of human *expression* and, as such, so it should be judged. If we look upon craft merely as skill, with no consideration of feeling other than pride or enjoyment in a job well done, then we must, surely, look to the complete process, involving mind and spirit in unison with hands communicating through the finished piece, as the key to ceramic art.

As Bernard Leach once wrote: "We are searching for a balanced form of self-expression, and potting is one of the few activities in which a person can use his natural facilities of head, heart and hand in balance".

I have used the male gender throughout this book in any general observations purely for reasons of economy. Likewise, in the context of this book words such as 'artist', 'craftsman', 'potter', 'ceramist' and so on, should be read as synonymous, since I make no distinction between them and they relate to either sex.

I am indebted to all those potters who have so generously contributed to my research in so many helpful ways. Their illustrated works reveal a little of the enormous variety and versatility to be found in contemporary studio ceramics and provide us with a visual feast. Unless otherwise accredited all the quotations have been taken directly from the potters themselves.

Norwich 1983

White porcelain columns fired to 1380°C. Heights $8\frac{11}{16}$–$15\frac{3}{4}$in(22–40cm). These objects were deliberately shaped and deformed by hitting them and firing bullets through them. The artist describes his work as 'essentially the meeting of a civilised form/prism with an organic energy'. By IMRE SCHRAMMEL (Hungry), 1980.

'Dinner on the Grass'. Industrially-made bisque tiles, oxides with painted and poured coloured glazes fired to 1060°C. 18 × 24in (45.7 × 61cm). By MAGGIE BERKOWITZ (UK), 1974. In the collection of Simon Digby.

BELOW: 'Atlantide' beasts. Stoneware, modified extruded forms. Smallest beast is a porcelain whistle 3½in(8.9cm) long. Larger piece 12 × 8in (30.5 × 20.3cm). Fired in oxidation to cones 8–10. By MAURICE SAVOIE (Canada), 1977.

1 INTRODUCTION

Since the early 1950s we have witnessed a phenomenal rise in the numbers of people actively engaged in the crafts as practitioners, customers, materials and equipment suppliers, patrons, writers and administrators. This movement gained momentum in succeeding decades and mushroomed to become a multimillion-pound industry world-wide by the 1970s. More than any other medium, ceramics captured the imagination of a large proportion of those attracted to the crafts as a way of life. This impetus has not yet slackened and may well continue indefinitely.

The interest of potters and spectators alike has been stimulated and sustained by a host of major exhibitions of contemporary work over the past thirty years. Many public museums and galleries have established growing collections of all kinds of ceramics by living craftsmen. The International Academy of Ceramics has mounted memorable (and controversial) exhibitions at places as far afield as Prague, Istanbul, London and Calgary. Regional, national and international shows and symposia around the world are sponsored by a multitude of different organizations ranging from crafts councils and crafts societies to industrial concerns far too numerous to mention individually. This diverse involvement is indicative of the enormous self-generating enthusiasm for studio ceramics at the present time. The amount of literature available today in the form of books and magazines dealing with every conceivable aspect of the history, making, appreciation and criticism of ceramics is vast compared with the paucity of material to be found only three decades ago.

The number of practising potters at all levels has multiplied many times over during this period. From time to time it has been suggested that saturation point, at least as far as marketing was concerned, had been reached. Yet, the field has so far continued to expand. It appeared to be without bounds until the world economic recession of the 1970s undermined the somewhat fragile viability of a number of craft shops and galleries established in less stringent times.

Once the term 'craft' gained credibility in a sympathetic climate, it was not long before it became fashionable to call souvenir shops 'craft centres' or 'galleries'. Consequently, all manner of ill-conceived and badly executed rubbish, masquerading under a 'handmade' label, has been produced for an indiscriminate tourist market. On the other hand, specialist galleries, regularly supplied by their selected and named craftsmen, have catered for the growing appetites of more serious and discerning collectors. The term 'gallery' itself suggests the superior status normally associated with works of art and stresses the individual and original nature of the pieces displayed. This element of uniqueness has been emphasized further as the names of leading craftsmen have become known. Their particular styles were recog-

OPPOSITE: Figure vessel, hand-built, painted slips. Height 19in (48.3cm). By RUDY AUTIO (USA), 1980.

Three stoneware pots with incised decoration under wood-ash glazes. Height of tallest 12in (35cm). Reduction fired to 1300°C. By MICHAEL CASSON (UK), 1982.

nized and imitated quite early on during the period in question. In part this was due to the enthusiastic involvement of inspired individuals prepared to invest their faith, time and money in opening and maintaining craft galleries.

Since the end of the Second World War professional craft guilds and societies have been constituted regionally and nationally in many countries. They have all drawn upon their membership to provide advice and mutual support while promoting and attempting to raise the standards of craftsmanship in all its senses. They have made efforts to educate the public in a variety of ways. The Craftsmen Potters Association (CPA) has been the driving force in Britain since its foundation in 1957. Like most professional societies, the CPA has a highly selective list of full members as its core around which a large associate (non-selective) membership is encouraged to participate in its activities. The Potters Society of Australia, The British Columbia Potters Guild, The New Zealand Society of Potters and many others have all made enormous contributions towards improving the status and accessibility of ceramics.

Publicly funded bodies have been formed to meet the rapidly growing demands for material support and recognition of the crafts in general. The American Crafts Council, the Crafts Council of Australia, the Canadian Crafts Council, the Crafts Council in Britain and other similar organizations, together with the World Crafts Council, now seek to promote and preserve the crafts and to provide material assistance in the form of grants and loans.

A number of discernible factors have fuelled the current crafts revival and boosted ceramics in particular. The most important of these is associated with what might be called the search for human identity in a world where machines and technological developments distance the individual from creative thought and action, the maker has become overshadowed by the consumer; a situation foreseen by John Ruskin, William Morris and others over a century ago.

It is difficult to estimate the degree to which television programmes on the crafts or the teaching of art and crafts in schools have brought greater awareness of the environment and a fresh respect for things made by hand. Indeed, any claim must be tempered by reference to wider issues influencing social change. The therapeutic

RIGHT: Large covered jar in porcelain with variegated glaze. Height 20in (55.9cm), width 10in (25.4cm). Reduction fired to cone 9 with propane gas in a 55cu.ft trolley kiln. By TOM TURNER (USA).

Small porcelain bottle, carved with iris design under a celadon glaze. Height 3½in (8.9cm). Fired to cone 11. By SCOTT MALCOLM (USA), 1982.

'Edwardian Rocking Horse'. Stoneware (St Thomas's body), thrown and modelled elements. Height 8in (23cm). Fired to 1280°C. For some of his pieces HILARY BROCK uses a glaze containing 50 parts wood ash and 50 parts china clay (with added oxides in small quantities) under another glaze mixture of 20 parts feldspar: 40 parts china clay; and 40 parts whiting. By HILARY BROCK (UK), 1981.

Stoneware jar with three lugs, oak-ash glaze over red slip engraved with tree pattern. Height 16in (40.6cm). Reduction fired to 1320°C. By JIM MALONE (UK), 1982.

Stoneware bowl decorated with iron oxide and cobalt, with iron chromate on clay matt glaze containing rutile, applied thinly. Diameter 12in (30.5cm). The body of this piece is a blend of ball clays (with Staffordshire red marl added to tint) with refractory grog and sand. Reduction fired to 1280°C. By HENRY HAMMOND (UK), 1979.

benefits of creative activity for the release of stress, coupled with the immense personal satisfaction to be gained through practical work, certainly encouraged many people to enrol for leisure classes in pottery. The subject provides an ideal opportunity to work a material in the raw state from the conception of the idea through to the finished piece thus furnishing a complete, rewarding and meaningful exercise normally denied to the great majority in their everyday work.

A kind of romantic idealism has grown up around studio pottery. The rosy, soft-focus picture of a potter living in the tranquil countryside in a converted barn selling his wares direct to an appreciative, informed public has become a popular image. This romanticism grew out of the strong movement towards self-sufficiency: a desire to live off the land, harvesting the fruits of one's own labours. Environmental concerns, fears for ecological imbalance, the developing lobby for conservation and an obsession with organically grown health foods were all indicators of the underlying social trends encouraging handmade domestic wares to flourish. The natural, earthy character of such pieces, which were often only partially glazed, was further emphasized by brown and oatmeal colours. Their unassuming presence evokes less hectic times in tune with the search for what might be termed the spiritual essence of life.

It was a mood taken up and exploited by the advertising industry and by film and television producers. Nostalgia for things past was, and still is, encouraged by numerous sentimental advertisements, while documentary television programmes and period plays add to the illusion that salvation can be found in the backward glance.

Studio pottery also offered quiet relief from the somewhat frenetic cacophony of crude colours used to decorate industrial ceramics with 'contemporary' patterns after the war. It is difficult to distinguish specific national styles in studio ceramics today because ease of travel and rapid communication of ideas tend to blur the picture. Technological developments are quickly taken up and trends of fashion likewise.

Porcelain bowl decorated with cobalt, iron and manganese oxides with rutile over a satin matt dolomite glaze. Diameter 6in (15.2cm). Reduction fired to 1280°C. By PETER LANE (UK), 1980.

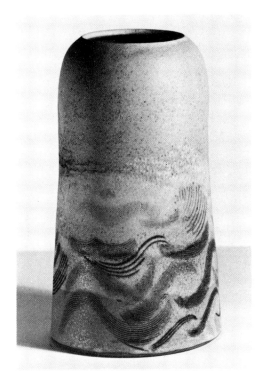

FAR LEFT: Stoneware pot with inlaid slip decoration (inspired by sea movements) under two glazes. Height 12in (30.5cm). Fired in oxidation to 1250°C. By EILEEN LEWENSTEIN (UK), 1982.

LEFT: 'Corinthian'. Porcelain jar with metallic lustre glaze, once fired. Height $11\frac{13}{16}$in (30cm). By ROBIN HOPPER (Canada), 1981.

Potters gain their inspiration from diverse sources, and few can remain totally immune and isolated from the continuous bombardment of ideas from without. A large number of studio potters are content to work within a limited frame of reference without engaging in radical changes of style or content. Innovation for its own sake is insufficient. What may seem vitally new and exciting today often appears shallow and shabby tomorrow. Fashions are as transitory in decorative art as they are in those ceramics which aspire to the status of fine art. The latter term is often an excuse for bad workmanship, as if the craft component in some way contaminates the expressive element. On the other hand, really good craftsmanship is more likely to be balanced by evidence of feeling and genuine human expression. It seems to me that respect, indeed love, for clay itself coupled with the sensitive use of technique cannot be completely divorced from the expressive content of the work.

The unusual, the avant-garde, the bizarre, even the whimsical are more likely to attract comment and publicity, yet there still remains a universal appeal in the personal interpretations of those basic vessel forms which have stood the test of time. Such forms will continue to challenge and fascinate potters as long as clay is available to them.

Regardless of country or cultural

Stoneware pedestal bowl with unglazed band of oxide and white glazes. Diameter 12in (30.5cm). Reduction fired to 1300°C. The basic glaze recipe is 25 parts china clay; 50 parts potash feldspar; 20 parts whiting; 5 parts mixed wood ash (unwashed, 40s mesh). By ROBIN WELCH (UK), 1981.

Group of stoneware
forms, press-moulded,
colours brown to black.
Height of tallest 6in
(15.2cm). Fired in
electric kiln to 1280°C.
By GEOFFREY SWINDELL
(UK), 1974.

background, countless variations are possible within any category of wheel-thrown form, for example. Infinite adjustments can be made in the relationship of rim or lip to neck, to shoulder, to belly or to foot. The profile, proportions and volume of a pot can, together, communicate feelings of varying intensity. They may suggest strength, weakness, tension, serenity, flamboyance, reserve, exuberance, severity, humour, elegance, gentleness or contemplation. Such qualities in a pot often defy precise definition but, even among a number of thrown pieces of similar shape judged by any group of potters, a good piece which 'succeeds' will be instinctively recognized. The addition of colour, glaze or some other form of surface treatment increases the range of possibilities to the point where a lifetime could be spent exploring what at first glance appears to be but a simple theme.

With such a long tradition of vessel-making behind them, it might be thought impossible that potters working on the wheel can have anything to add to all that has gone before. Merely copying forms from another time, place or culture is certain to be a sterile occupation. The potter's personal feeling for the shapes he makes and the sensitivity with which he fashions them will condition the expressive content of each piece and, whether good or bad, make it unique. The individual style, perhaps even the personality of the potter, may be recognized in the bottle, jar, vase or bowl as much as in a sculptural object.

Hand-building methods allow a still freer interpretation of the vessel's profile even though the form may often remain basically round in section.

Truly original potters are, nevertheless, rare spirits. Most commentators could agree on the names of a handful of major influential figures in twentieth-century studio ceramics who have given fresh impetus by their example. They are, in the main, numbered among those innovators who abandoned utilitarian pieces. But the dominant force world-wide has undoubtedly been **Bernard Leach**. For some time, any conflict with his tenets amounted almost to heresy. *A Potter's Book*, published by Leach in 1940, is still widely read. This was the first book of its kind and it has had an enormous impact on potters due to the comprehensive way in which Leach dealt with the philosophical and technical aspects of ceramics. His other writings and teachings in many countries also gathered thousands of disciples.

In Britain, the Leach way was to be challenged during a period of student unrest, dissatisfaction and, ultimately, revolution against established traditions in the 1960s. Conventional teaching methods and patterns of art education in colleges at this time were called into question. The way was cleared for new ideas concerning processes, content, and purpose, to be developed. Freed from concentration upon wheelmade pottery forms, a new generation of craftsmen began to explore hand-building methods. Industrial techniques such as slip-casting, sand-blasting and screen-printing, hitherto shunned by studio potters, were increasingly exploited. This sudden liberalization released a veritable explosion of creative energy. Ceramics became the vehicle for adventurous expression with a new vitality unfettered by utilitarian constraints.

Hans Coper was one of the outstanding teachers in Britain whose attitudes and supreme mastery of ceramic form strongly influenced this emerging generation. Some of these, like **Geoffrey Swindell, Elizabeth Fritsch, Glenys Barton** and **Alison Britton**, achieved international recognition during the 1970s.

Ruth Duckworth's uninhibited approach to clay also made a tremendous impact at this time through her teaching and personal work in Britain and America, while **Lucie Rie** and **James Tower** in their individual

Stoneware pot, oxidised stoneware with matt black (manganese) surface. Made by joining thrown forms. Height $8\frac{5}{16}$in (21.2cm). By HANS COPER (UK), 1972.

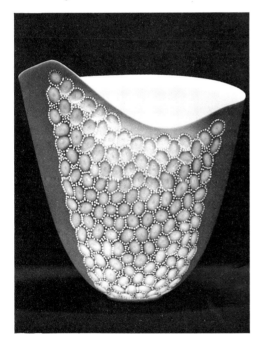

ABOVE: Bone china form, slip-cast, with semi-pierced and pierced section and transparent glaze. Height $2\frac{1}{2}$in (7cm). By ANGELA VERDON (UK), 1982.

RIGHT: Stoneware pot, oxidised stoneware made from several thrown elements joined together. $14\frac{1}{4} \times 12 \times 4$in (36.2 × 30.5 × 10.2cm). By HANS COPER (UK), 1972.

ways influenced developments by their teaching and example.

In the United States it was to be the appearance of 'Funk' ceramics during the 1960s, with its 'low-brow humour', poking fun at social and sexual taboos in brutal figurative imagery, that was to overturn popular conceptions and stake claims for a traditional craft medium in the field of fine arts. The 'truth to materials approach' held dear by the vast majority of practising potters was irrelevant to these artists. Surrealism and super-realism created in clay and glaze seemed doubly shocking since the materials were totally subordinate to the idea which gave rise to the object.

The physical transformation of clay into ceramics became merely a step along the way rather than an integral contributive element. Evidence of recognizable ceramic qualities, inherent in the nature of the material, was often disguised or hidden as it was not considered relevant to the overall concept. Nuances of glaze or surface texture used with the specific intention of complementing form were likewise unimportant. It was as if all respect for clay as a

RIGHT: Stoneware pot, hand-built, with washes of copper, nickel and iron oxides under two glazes, fired to 1280°C. Height 15in (38.1cm). By RUTH DUCKWORTH (USA), 1978.

ABOVE: Stoneware cup, hand-built, with low-fire glazes and photographic decals. Height 7in (17.8cm). By ERIK GRONBORG (USA), 1981.

Earthenware dish, press-moulded, sgraffito through glaze; purple, black and white. 20 × 15in (50.8 × 38.1cm). By JAMES TOWER (UK), 1979.

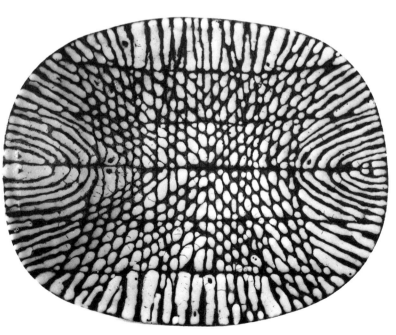

material, together with its associated traditions, had been totally abandoned. Indeed, some critics argued that the work might just as well have been executed in wood, metal or plastics.

Until the 1950s, American potters had tended to follow formalist European directions in which the processes were not required to contribute to the ceramic object other than to provide the means by which it was made. This attitude placed much discernible emphasis upon high-quality craftsmanship, but it was to be disturbed by an alternative set of aesthetic values emanating from Japan. Here again, it was **Bernard Leach** who provided the initial bridge from East to West propagating Zen aestheticism concerned with what he called the "fundamental elements" breathing life into pots: "inner harmony, nobility, purity, strength, breadth and generosity, or even exquisiteness and charm". According to these values intuitive performance takes precedence over intellectual principles of design and assumes greater importance in relation to those traditional European concepts involving purely visual aspects of form. The completed works could, therefore, be viewed as no more than the tangible evidence or record of the *creative action* that brought them into existence. Artists approaching ceramics with this

ABOVE RIGHT: Earthenware form with painted slips, thrown and cut, unglazed. Height $11\frac{13}{16}$in (30cm). Fired to 1020°C. VILMA HENKELMAN's work is fired "as low as possible to stay close to the authenticity of the material". She enjoys the physical activity of making pieces in clay and really feels that the work is complete 'before' firing. She feels sorry to have to fire pots because she feels they are at their most beautiful when freshly made and still wet. By VILMA HENKELMAN (Holland), 1982.

'Fragmented Cube'. Slab construction. Glaze: verdigris crater with heavy drops, fired in oxidation. $9\frac{5}{16} \times 8\frac{7}{8}$in (23.6 × 22.5cm). By OTTO NATZLER (USA), 1979.

philosophy were not bound by normally accepted standards of craftsmanship. Artistic freedom was paramount.

Nevertheless, functionalism continues to dominate the popular view of ceramics. It is the tap-root from which pottery forms have grown naturally, neither imitating nor representing, nor even suggesting, anything other than their own existence or purpose.

New directions are often the result of individual brilliance. Artists, with vision and the conviction that they have something worth saying, break the bounds of established norms. Their personality and dynamism stimulate reappraisal and provoke responses. They assume a questioning, probing role, refusing to conform. Others, following in their footsteps, may find their own new directions. Moral courage is a requisite whenever fresh ground is broken, especially where the outcome is unclear and the technology uncertain.

Sometimes, postwar ceramics have been swept along in the slipstream of contemporary movements in painting and sculpture with international repercussions. While Europe at large remained preoccupied with ceramic vessels, utilitarian or otherwise, American potters were responding to a wave of Abstract Expressionism led by energetic innovators like **Peter Voulkos, Rudy Autio, Ron Nagle, Kenneth Price, Robert Arneson** and others.

Arneson is one of the major survivors of the influential Funk style of the 1960s in which form, whether good or bad, was only incidental to contextual issues. Shattering all preconceptions of good taste, and often relying on the element of shock similar to that achieved by Dada and Surrealist art, it was a movement that attracted many followers, although its impact was mainly confined to America. With a few exceptions, European potters kept their distance and continued to exploit the nature of ceramic materials by creating forms either specifically related to function or with a strong affinity to the vessel as object. For many of them, intellectual preoccupation with visual elements such as form, volume, tension, movement, rhythm, the relationship of insides to outsides, and the texture or surface treatment of pottery vessels, has remained the common core. Similarly, natural forms, patterns and textures, rather than issues arising from the human condition, social comment or modern painting, have continued to provide the major references in Western European ceramics.

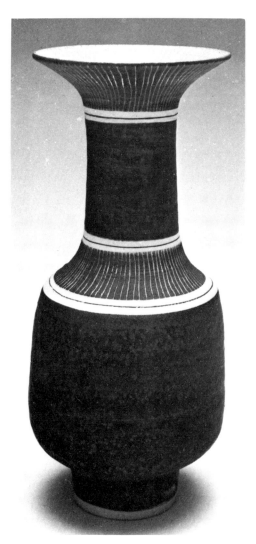

RIGHT: RUDY AUTIO (USA) working in a positive, uninhibited manner, on a hand-built form in the plastic state with linear drawing through painted slips, 1982.

Bottle vase, oxidised porcelain, mainly blue with horizontal bands of bronze (copper and manganese oxides) and sgraffito decoration through to porcelain body. Height 8½in (21.5cm). By LUCIE RIE (UK). In the Crafts Council Collection.

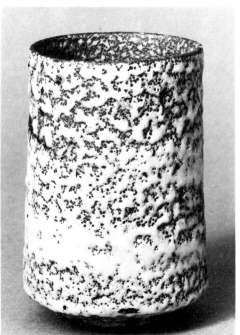

Pot, oxidised stoneware with thickly applied glaze over dark body. Height 6¾in (17.2cm). By LUCIE RIE (UK), 1960. In the Crafts Council Collection.

Most of the potters illustrated in this book reflect this European attitude irrespective of their origins. Few are concerned with the *double entendre*, the visual pun or the *trompe l'oeil* of their American West Coast contemporaries. Traditional forms of pottery still provide a springboard for a kind of disciplined personal enquiry which is infinite. (This concern for visual and tactile perfection combined with subtle, evocative, yet reserved emotional content can be seen in the work of potters such as **Karl Scheid, Lucie Rie, Alev Siesbye, Catherine Hiersoux, Gotlind Weigel** and **Geoffrey Swindell.**)

Where traditions have been transplanted (rather than inherited) into an emerging culture, adjustments, inevitably, have to be made. When local materials have to be discovered and adapted for use, any attempt to forge cultural identity also requires resourcefulness and a capacity for invention. Early work may well be full of second-hand,

ABOVE: Porcelain bowl with iron and manganese feldspathic glaze. Unglazed band with incised linear decoration stained with iron oxide, reduction fired to 1360°C. Height 3¼in (8cm). By KARL SCHEID (West Germany), 1981.

RIGHT: Porcelain bottle vase. Height 10in (25.4cm). Reduction fired to cones 10–11. This pot is made in two parts, the neck being thrown on top of the leather-hard base. By CATHERINE HIERSOUX (USA), 1982.

ABOVE: Porcelain cylindrical form, with slip and glaze-resist bands. Height 6⅛in (15.5cm). Reduction fired to 1360°C. By URSULA SCHEID (West Germany), 1981.

RIGHT: 'Pebble form'. Stoneware with layered feldspathic glazes and iron oxide, reduction fired to 1360°C. Height 8⅝in (22cm). By GOTLIND WEIGEL (West Germany), 1980.

derivative imagery, but a host of local factors give fresh impetus for experiment and contribute towards the distillation and reappraisal of attitudes.

Specific national styles are difficult to identify because the individual approaches in each country are so great. Nevertheless, it is possible to obtain a 'flavour' which might be associated with certain national characteristics and qualities differing from one country or region to another. In particular, relatively young ceramics communities are likely to be made up of immigrants from a variety of cultural backgrounds. These groups often feed upon the traditions of Europe and the Far East, but they are increasingly influenced by ideas powerfully fermented in the United States. A continuous interchange of potters conducting teaching workshops also contributes to the expansion of knowledge and opportunity.

In Australian ceramics, for example, a combination of external influences can be

ABOVE: Stoneware bowl, with charcoal-black pegmatite glaze and lighter areas unglazed, coil-built, and fired to 1300°C in an electric kiln. Diameter 13¾in (35cm). By ALEV SIESBYE (Denmark), 1980.

Stoneware jar with blue matt glaze, thrown in two sections. Height 19¹¹⁄₁₆in (50cm). By ALAN PEASCOD (Australia), 1981.

ABOVE: 'Dragon' pots. Porcelain thrown and
modelled, celadon glazed in heavy reduction to
1300°C in a natural gas-fired kiln. Height $6\frac{11}{16}$in
(17cm). By ANNE MERCER (Australia), 1981.

Two discoid forms, stoneware, with high
magnesium crackled glaze and oxided,
textured surface. Height of taller form $11\frac{7}{16}$in
(29cm). By DEREK SMITH (Australia), 1981.

'Clouds'. Panel in unglazed, sand-blasted porcelain and acrylic, with graphic treatment on acrylic, drypoint etched and sand-blasted. Height 24in (61cm). By ALAN WATT (Australia), 1981.

identified. But, having absorbed so much from outside, stimulus and inspiration are now coming from within. This may, in part, be the product of a search for self-sufficiency and a recognition of national identity. There is certainly evidence of a rather special kind of quality that is difficult to define: fruits of an adventurous, carefree attitude applied with energy, vitality and enthusiasm. Regional potters' societies are hyperactive in the country encouraging vigorous experiment. Unlike British potters, who take for granted the easy availability of reliable, commercially prepared materials, many Australians prospect their own clays, rocks and minerals. Some have had few other options open to them. The intimate knowledge and confidence gained through this activity have helped to free many from the kind of traditional straitjacket that can inhibit their European counterparts. There can be no doubt that the so-called limitations of materials and techniques are being seriously challenged through the raw, almost brutal, approach of some studio potters in Australia.

LEFT: 'Southerly Buster'. Cup and saucer in stoneware, hand-modelled and thrown with underglazes and oxides under matt and glossy glazes. Width 10¼in (26cm), height 7⅞in (20cm), depth 5⅞in (15cm). Fired in an electric kiln. 'Southerly buster' is an Australian term describing southerly storms which blow up quickly and are quite fearsome. The theme of the cup and saucer is one that I work on seriously from time to time. It is most utilitarian as the cup is stable and practical for the early morning cup of tea. The toast fits neatly between the palm trees, while the boiled egg snuggles comfortably among the waves. By SANDRA TAYLOR (Australia).

2 DESIGN SOURCES

What are the attractions of working in clay? The technology alone appears to be so daunting. Frustration and disappointment are promised more often than in any other medium. Each stage, from the plastic state through to the final firing, carries particular hazards threatening the survival of every object.

The potter cannot retain the kind of close control of his work *as it develops* that a painter or a weaver can. He is physically distanced from each piece when it is committed to the kiln. Clays, glazes, oxides and stains undergo drastic transformation when fired so that the potter must visualise the ultimate colours and surfaces likely to be revealed after firing and when the kiln has cooled. He cannot tell exactly if he has correctly judged the weight and distribution of colour or the thickness of glaze until the kiln is unpacked. It may still be possible to retrieve pieces which have failed technically or aesthetically by re-glazing and firing again, perhaps several times, until a more satisfactory result is achieved, but I doubt if any serious potter would claim to have had one hundred per cent success every time. Many are far more likely to have destroyed pieces that represented hours of careful work but which failed for one reason or another not entirely within their control.

Despite these disadvantages, clay as a material, together with the processes through which it must pass in becoming ceramic, appeals to the artist-craftsman through the versatility which allows it to be fashioned in various ways. Its tactile qualities from wet to dry to fired are unique. Its texture may be anything from coarse and granular to smooth and fine. Each type of clay and every stage of its working offers countless options, while suggesting specific or possible applications. Their deep involvement with the physical properties and

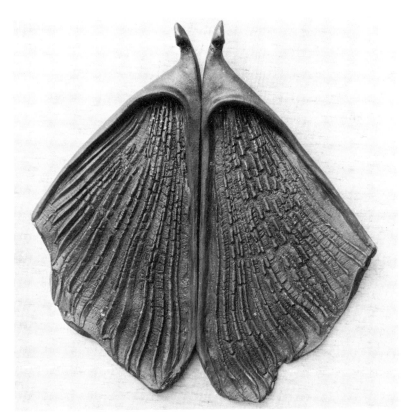

ABOVE: 'Gemini Series No. 19'. Wall sculpture, stoneware with burnished oxide finish on the rolled, scraped and stretched form, reduction fired to Orton cone 9. Height $20\frac{1}{16}$in(51cm), width $16\frac{1}{2}$in(42cm). By IAN FIRTH (New Zealand), 1982

OPPOSITE ABOVE: 'Pleasure Patio'. Wall panel, porcelain coloured with oxides and body stains, slab-built. Size $13\frac{3}{4} \times 17\frac{3}{4}$in(35 × 45cm). The image is created by inlaying the coloured clays into carved and incised areas which are then scraped back to reveal the design. Slips and underglazes are also used and on some pieces colour is applied with an airbrush. The main slab is fired (unglazed) once to 1250°C in an electric kiln. Smaller components are inlaid, painted with slip, glazed and fired separately (and then, perhaps, enamelled or lustred) before being assembled. By LORRAINE LEE (Australia), 1982.

OPPOSITE BELOW: 'Ma-Me-O Beach'. Wall panel, porcelain $12\frac{5}{8} \times 16\frac{1}{2} \times 2\frac{3}{8}$in (32 × 42 × 6cm). 'The beach is a dominant feature of life on the coast of Australia. These pieces are essentially decorative, escapist and probably reflective of my own rather hedonistic nature.' By LORRAINE LEE (Australia), 1982.

techniques of the ceramic medium provides a common ground for endless discussion among potters. The shared experience and the risks involved encourage strong affinities between them and promote an understanding across the usual barriers of language.

The ease with which a lump of plastic clay can be shaped and re-shaped by pinching, pulling, twisting, tearing, rolling and impressing satisfies quite basic instincts, as anyone who has watched a young child making mud pies will understand. Such responsiveness, inherent in clay, arouses sensations which stimulate creative thought, so that its particular character alone may be the starting-point for both functional and non-functional work. Later stages and techniques used in the process of conversion into the ceramic state may also trigger ideas to be explored. Occasionally, chance will provide those opportunities. There is always a feeling of excitement, of nervous anticipation, in firing, especially when risks have been taken and hunches played. Surprising colour combinations or visual textures from the interaction of glaze and body ingredients, for example, may bring delight or disappointment.

The most experienced and long-lived potters confess to feelings of suspense, even impatience, when awaiting the cooling of a kiln. I have felt both intense elation and deepest despair on opening a kiln. In this context probably only potters, professional or amateur, can fully appreciate such feelings. The surprises, delights and disappointments of a child's Christmas stocking make a rather tame analogy to this experience.

Certainly, the variables involved in the creation of ceramics present us with almost infinite scope, although committing the product of hours of labour to the sometimes uncertain effects of extreme heat is an unavoidable act of faith, hope, and even love. This aspect of ceramics has changed very little over the centuries. It forms part of the attraction of the medium, as does the continuity of a long tradition. In no other medium is the modern artist so obsessed with materials and processes or with the achievements of past generations. Indeed, some leading potters find their inspiration entirely within an historical framework. Their work is nonetheless a worthy part of the contemporary scene.

The development of a personal visual language in ceramics is normally dependent upon the potter reaching the point where technical aspects become a familiar, natural and unforced part of the creative act. Regardless of what form emerges, and for any number of reasons, the artist who chooses clay does so because for him it is the most appropriate medium through which to express feelings.

While the initial stimulus for the work is sometimes perfectly clear, it may also come from an indefinable variety of experiences or an amalgam of sensory information stored in the subconscious. Whether sources of imagery can be easily traced or not, a further transformation and adjustment will have taken place in realizing their substance in ceramic form.

Often the work will be in direct response to visual stimuli in the environment. Landscapes, plants, animals, human figures and other elements from the natural world provide the starting-point for the great majority of potters. This may be a conscious interpretation of observed phenomena or an attempt to express the spirit of time and place; to distil its essence.

The 'flash of inspiration' which seemingly materialises 'out of nowhere' is unlikely to be a regular occurrence, and certainly not one to be relied upon. But there is a delicious, semi-conscious condition between sleeping and waking when the mind roams freely. Random images, juxtaposed, not always focused, come and go. I have (on rare occasions) experienced such an early-morning state, bringing with it an amazing

Stoneware bowl, coil-built, with copper-ash glaze and in part with a cobalt blue feldspathic glaze, fired to 1220°C in oxidation. Height $10\frac{5}{8}$in(27cm). By HANS DE JONG (Holland), 1981.

clarity. Problems which had seemed insoluble are often resolved in the simplest way. This animation cannot be instituted at will and is, unfortunately, an infrequent happening.

New Zealand potter, **Ian Firth**, described to me a similar experience when for him "ideas flow in that delightful half-state between dream and reality *before* sleep. When the creative part of the brain seems to be super-active, and the mind virtually surfs on an ocean of ideas . . . wonderful, flickering images. Pad and pencil become essential bedtime equipment".

Few people can rely on such bonuses of inspiration. Work is more likely to evolve through the balance of intellect and sensibility. Alertness to exploit occasional unexpected qualities of surface and form to good effect is a further very useful attribute.

Continuous exploration of a particular aspect of form by individual potters makes a fascinating study. Their work presents us with a fairly straightforward task in ident-

ifying their personal styles and interests.

Among those who work within the European tradition and who express themselves in pure vessel forms that undergo constant refinement, is **Geoffrey Swindell** (UK). For several years he has concentrated upon exploring a theme of small porcelain pots rising from precariously tiny bases. Their physical vulnerability is part of the attraction for him. He feels that they should be cosseted to be enjoyed. He has discovered seemingly infinite variety of profile while keeping his shapes within fairly narrow confines. Subtle changes of direction, shifting the relationship of sharp, skirt-like flanges to crisply defined curves, in one piece after another ensure that no two pieces are the same, yet their origin is unmistakable. He claims his roots to be firmly in the English ceramic tradition of Thomas Wheildon, the eighteenth century Staffordshire potter, and others; a natural-enough feeling for one born and brought up in the industrial pottery town of Stoke-on-Trent. Much of the initial stimulus for these forms came

Porcelain pot, thrown and turned with airbrushed copper carbonate bands under a dolomite glaze. Height 4in(10.2cm). The crackled glaze pattern has been stained with a commercially prepared gold lustre in a third firing. By GEOFFREY SWINDELL (UK), 1981.

Stoneware form, wheel-thrown elements joined and modified. By HANS COPER (UK). In the Crafts Council Collection.

from his collection of tin toys, sea shells and plastic objects. This skilful and fastidious attention to detail in his ceramics has also been useful to him in modelling an extremely convincing 'Space Station' from oddments of plastic kits and fragments of plastic containers. Handling such objects made from different materials has certainly stimulated ideas, but the impetus for Geoffrey Swindell's work is sustained by a searching re-examination of the basic elements of line, rhythm, form, proportion, colour and surface in combination.

Swindell shares this concern for the control of formal design elements with one of his teachers, **Hans Coper**, who is undoubtedly a major figure in twentieth-century ceramics. Coper's influence, especially in Europe, has been, and will continue to be, considerable. Born in Germany in 1920, his untimely death in the summer of 1981 deprived the pottery world of a unique artist and highly respected teacher.

Coper's pots have a monumental presence irrespective of their size. Indeed, some are very small, no more than a few inches high, often tapering down to a sharp point balanced upon a tiny plinth. His larger pieces, with overlaid, brushed slips and oxides, have rich tactile qualities; their positive, unpretentious shapes are imbued with a quiet strength. The interplay of verticals, horizontals and diagonals in cylindrical, spherical and ovoid forms, allied to subtle proportional changes, makes any exhibition of Coper's work a kind of visual symphony.

Stoneware pot, elongated body consisting of tapering neck set in conical form on a solid base, with slip applied and burnished. All forms wheel-thrown, joined and modified. Height $8\frac{5}{16}$in(21.2cm). By HANS COPER (UK).

Bottle, oxidised porcelain with sgraffito
through brushed oxides to porcelain body.
Height 11¾in(29.8cm). By LUCIE RIE (UK).

It is almost impossible to mention Hans
Coper without thinking of **Lucie Rie** with
whom he shared ideals and a workshop for
several years. Like Coper's, Lucie Rie's work
challenged the Anglo-Oriental aestheticism
of the Leach school. The intuitive evolution
of her work was admirably demonstrated in
a retrospective exhibition held in England in
1981/2, to mark her eightieth birthday. Her
most recent pieces displayed on this occa-
sion were superb examples of the potter's art.
Form, surface, colour, pattern and texture in
exquisite harmony revealed a positive approach allied to a gentleness that suggests a
degree of inner serenity few ever achieve.
Recurring themes in the shape of bowls,
bottles and vases continue to provide this
remarkable potter with opportunities for an
infinite range of expression.

Derek Smith (Australia) is another potter
who makes pieces in stoneware and porcelain with clean, precise profiles developed
from cylinders, circles, cones and spheres.
He is something of a perfectionist and highly
critical of his own personal work. Running a
production workshop in Sydney, he feels
that the time spent on personal work is
worthwhile and valuable to him but it is not
easy to find. "It remains a delicate balance of
sound business management and creative
indulgence." The composition of colour and
texture, point and line on a particular form
presents him with infinite avenues of exploration around a chosen theme, while altered
proportions create new emphases in a group
of related forms.

OPPOSITE RIGHT: Stoneware bowl, part glazed and banded with oxides on heavily grogged body. Height 9in(22.9cm). Reduction fired to 1300°C. By ROBIN WELCH (UK), 1981.

RIGHT: Flat bottle, stoneware, slab construction, grey-blue celadon glaze with skinning melt fissures, fire marks and iridescence, reduction fired. Height 19⅞in(50.5cm). By OTTO NATZLER (USA), 1979.

BELOW RIGHT: Pedestal bowl, 'T' material with porcelain slip, stoneware reduction fired to 1300°C, satin white glaze. Height 8in(23cm). By JENNY WELCH (UK), 1981.

Recognizably functional pieces supply the starting-point for many potters whose prime aim nonetheless is to create visual and tactile interest rather than to satisfy utilitarian norms. Some, like **Otto Natzler** (USA), clothe such pieces with an incredible variety and richness of glaze surfaces and colours.

A simple container form capable of wide interpretation is the bowl. **Robin Welch** (UK) uses a heavily grogged body for his powerfully thrown bowls. The coarse clay is allowed, even encouraged, to tear at the rim, while scored lines and positive horizontal ribbing emphasize this potter's vigorous approach in the forming process. His wife, **Jenny Welch**, on the other hand, chooses to work with porcelain. Although she also favours a tall foot-ring or stem for her pieces, together with an uneven rim, the effect is totally different.

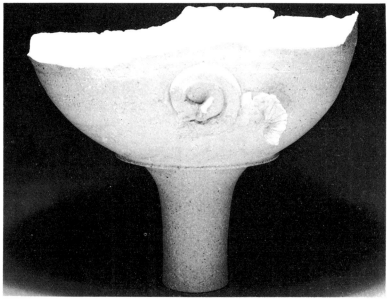

The rim of a bowl, that final edge, so often dictates the character of a piece. It is an element that holds endless fascination for potters like **Sally Bowen Prange** (USA). She cuts into the rim and re-applies the trimmed clay to transform an otherwise basic shape and create a less predictable piece that will invite more than a cursory glance.

Cutting away the top edge to produce a rhythmic, undulating line has been a feature of my own porcelain bowls for several years. The pleasure of throwing and turning porcelain is enhanced for me by the seductive nature of the material when it is carved at the leather-hard stage. In trying to trace the development of this interest in 'horizons', I remembered enjoying some Chinese bowls with foliate rims in the Ashmolean Museum, Oxford, during many visits there. This stimulus coupled with my love for the rolling landscape of the Berkshire Downs, the mountains of Cumbria and my collection of sea shells, somehow merge into feelings which find their natural, unforced expression in this form. Utilitarian considerations are irrelevant here.

RIGHT: SALLY BOWEN PRANGE (USA) working on her 'edgescape' vessels, 1982.

LEFT: Stoneware bowl, hand-thrown with calcium-barium glaze fired to 1300°C in a reduction atmosphere. Diameter 7⅞in(20cm). By VOLKER ELLWANGER (West Germany) 1981.

Alev Sieshye (Denmark) is not consciously concerned with function either, although she often explores the form of the bowl. Her pieces are coil-built and usually very large. She makes these pots with crisply defined profiles. She feels much more "part of the form" when hand-building in this way and on this scale. It is, she says, "a different feeling from working on a bowl which can fit into the palm of the hand. One really fights and has a dialogue going on when making a large piece. One learns so much from one's mistakes (*they* become very large too!)". She feels attached in a way to the ancient culture of Anatolia, her former homeland, but she finds it difficult to pinpoint a specific source of inspiration arising out of this connection. "Inspiration," she says, "is a whole life. Anything that moves us (poetry, music, art, any situation in any street, nature, human relationships, and so on) may be reflected in one's work."

Bowl, stoneware, hand-built with coils, decorated with olive-green glaze, fired to 1300°C in an electric kiln. Diameter 9$\frac{7}{16}$in(24cm). By ALEV SIESBYE (Denmark), 1976. In the collection of Museum Boymans-van Beuningen, Rotterdam.

Sheila Fournier (UK) has hand-built some handsome layered bowls the origins of which appear to be organic. Dry glazes poured in differing thicknesses complement these forms and contribute to their visual and tactile appeal. In pursuing this idea she has created a uniquely personal statement.

It is inevitable that the natural world should provide the most consistent source of stimulus for the overwhelming majority of potters. The enormous diversity of their responses in terms of ceramic objects and imagery continues to grow. The delicate bowls made by Mary Rogers (UK) in pinched porcelain are sometimes layered also but, in this case, the thin walls are crumpled and overlapped allowing varying degrees of translucency rather like the folded petals of a poppy flower that has not fully opened.

ABOVE: Bowl, hand-built in grogged stoneware with turquoise copper glaze, fired to 1260°C. Diameter 12in(30.5cm) approx. By SHEILA FOURNIER (UK).

James Tower (UK) makes sculptural objects which have their origins in an amalgam of natural phenomena: landscape, marine forms, tidal patterns and the flow of water, the ephemeral movement of waves and spray, the night sky, snow falling through light. The human torso has prompted some of his largest and most impressive pieces. Their simple shapes present a broad, uncluttered expanse for surface treatment, designs for which are abstracted and adapted to suit the forms.

'Beach'. Press-moulded earthenware form, sgraffito through greenish glaze over white tin glaze, fired to 1100°C. 22 × 13in(55.9 × 33cm). By JAMES TOWER (UK), 1980.

OPPOSITE BELOW: 'Folded Striped Form'. Hand-built porcelain. Height 5in (12.2cm). The overlapping folds in the translucent porcelain have been painted with broken green stripes on white to emphasize changes of direction inherent in folded fabric. Fired in an electric kiln. By MARY ROGERS (UK), 1980.

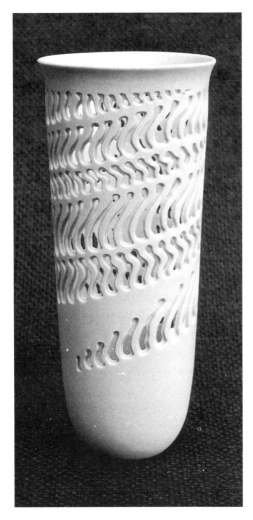

Porcelain vase, slip-cast, carved, sand-blasted and polished. Height 7in(17.7cm). Oxidised firing to 1240°C. By ALAN WHITTAKER (UK), 1982.

Suite of lace-like totems in porcelain and acrylic, slip-trailed within plaster moulds, unglazed, neutral, gas firing to 1300°C. Height of tallest 28in(71.1cm). By ALAN WATT (Australia), 1981.

'The Wave'. Translucent, unglazed porcelain on black acrylic base, neutral, gas firing to 1300°C. Height 4½in(11.4cm), width 9in(22.9cm). By ALAN WATT (Australia), 1981.

Alan Watt (Australia) gains most of his inspiration from the fringes of the Pacific Ocean. He hopes to capture the essence of coastal landscape and to reflect some of its particular characteristics in his work. He feels that porcelain enables him to express something of the delicate, fragile tracery found in certain forms of sea life; the whiteness of sun-bleached, skeletal remains; and the translucency and gossamer patterning of sun behind waves, rain and cloud. In this respect, he does not believe his work to be in any way conditioned by any specific culture or tradition, although he does acknowledge a very broad amalgam of contemporary influences from around the world.

Living and working at the edge of the Indian Ocean near Fremantle (Perth), **Joan Campbell** (Australia) finds that it is the horizon line of the sea interrupted by islands that is of absorbing interest to her. This has prompted her to make a series of sculptural pieces echoing her response to the initial stimulus and also to the materials and methods she uses in her work.

Eileen Lewenstein (UK) is another potter for whom the sea and beach are important sources of inspiration. From her home west of Hove on the South Coast of England she can look out over a pebble beach, divided by breakwaters, to the ever-changing surface of the English Channel perpetually in motion. Holes in flint, and chalk pebbles from the beach, suggested the indented or pierced cylindrical forms she has developed, while the movement of waves reflecting light has been expressed as painted glaze patterns on shallow, rectangular dishes.

ABOVE: 'Horizons'. Raku form. Height 11in(28cm) approx. Smoke-decorated with slip and seaweed. By JOAN CAMPBELL (Australia), 1981.

Two stoneware pots, thrown, pierced and modelled with inserted rod, glazed and oxidised to 1250°C. Height 9in(22.9cm) and 7in(17.7cm). By EILEEN LEWENSTEIN (UK), 1982.

'Landscape'. Stoneware form, textured area darkened with manganese slip. $10\frac{5}{8} \times 15\frac{3}{4}$in($27 \times 40$cm). Fired to $1300°$C in oxidation. By VERA VEHRING (West Germany), 1981.

Stoneware platter, with glaze painting of 'birds in landscape' using tenmoku, chun, rutile and copper-red glazes, fired by natural gas in a reduction atmosphere to $1300°$C. Diameter $15\frac{3}{8}$in(39cm). By BRYAN TRUEMAN (Australia), 1981.

Painting with glazes overlaid upon each other on the faces of large platters has provided several potters with the means to depict landscape in a fairly figurative way. The work of **Bryan Trueman** (Australia) reveals his training as a painter/printmaker adapted to harmonise with his self-taught skills as a potter. Although his subject matter is unashamedly pictorial landscape, the images are as likely to evolve through a series of methods in applying the glaze, as from direct observation.

For **Vera Vehring** (Germany) landscape suggests elements found in human form. Her slab-built pieces include textured areas picked out with dry iron and manganese oxides rubbed into the surface. **Yvette Mintzberg** (Canada) exploits the natural tendencies of clay to tear, crack and fold when worked in particular ways to express her response to aspects of landscape. She is intrigued by ice and rock formations which seem to combine much complexity of line with simplicity of form. She began climbing mountains and glaciers in 1975 and later spent some time in the Sinai desert. She believes that these are the experiences which have probably had the greatest influence on her work.

'Sunrise'. Smoke-fired stoneware form. $13\frac{1}{2} \times 8 \times 3$in ($34.3 \times 20.3 \times 7.6$cm). By YVETTE MINTZBERG (Canada), 1982.

'Earth'. Stoneware slab construction with manganese oxide in texture. $12 \times 14 \times 3$in ($30.5 \times 35.6 \times 7.6$cm). By YVETTE MINTZBERG (Canada), 1982.

'Leaf form'. Porcelain, hand built, 'veined' decoration with copper and manganese under a semi-matt white glaze. Height 6in(15.2cm). Fired in an electric kiln to 1280°C. By MARY ROGERS (UK), 1980.

Plants, seed-pods and fruits, shells, pebbles, bones and other natural objects have always provided endless ideas for forms and decoration. Many volumes could quite easily be devoted to this area of design alone. Clay can be readily shaped to resemble or suggest plant-like growth. **Mary Rogers** uses porcelain to capture the spirit of organic matter, while **Harlan House** (Canada) prefers to make a more literal interpretation, as seen in his 'Iris' series. These decorative pieces offset the ephemeral delicacy of the flowers against the lines of a picket fence.

Human figures modelled in clay through-out history tell us a great deal about the lives and customs of the people who made them. Some were created for religious purposes, others for purely ornamental reasons. Today, a number of ceramists take the figure as their starting-point for abstract sculpture, or to make some comment on the human condition, or the relationship of man to his environment. The images may be hauntingly sombre, humorous or whimsical. Some can be clearly recognized as falling within the realm of fine art, while others may be considered no more than decorative oddities: flights of fancy.

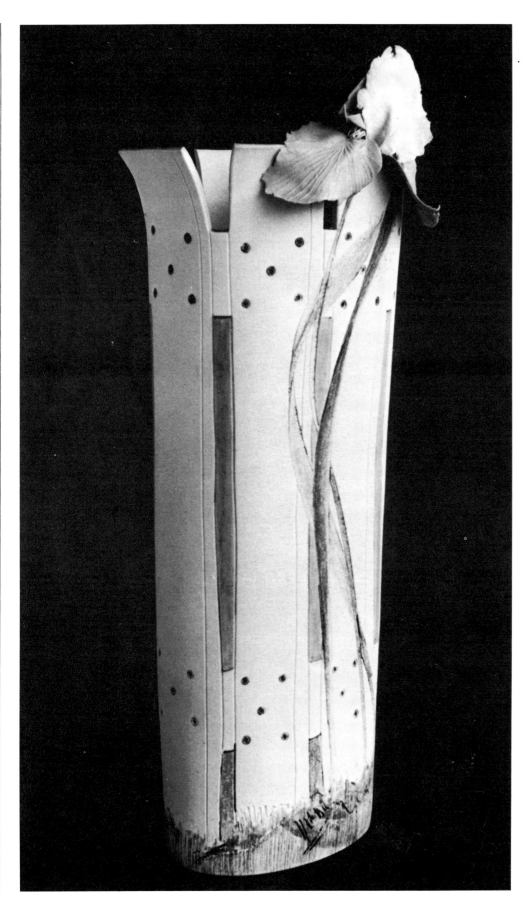

'Iris with Picket Fence'. Slip-cast porcelain vase with hand-modelled additions stamped, carved and incised with cobalt stains and chrome oxide brushwork. Height 18in(45.8cm). Once fired to cone 10. By HARLAN HOUSE (Canada), 1982.

Carmen Dionyse (Belgium) centres her work on the human figure and, above all, on the head and shoulders. Her imagery is powerfully symbolic, possessing an almost medieval mysticism. She is concerned with "form and content causally interrelated. Elements in connection with metaphysical and material creative urge. This genesis embodied in the phoenix symbol. Resurrection from the ashes of the fire of purification. Mother earth, source of all mineral and organic forms. The Janus principle in the experience of nature's rhythm (day and night). A mystical body of themes is created from improvisatory structuring in form and colour".

In Belgium, the Ministry of Commerce has provided considerable support for the country's artists at international exhibitions around the world. With no strong pottery background to inhibit their approach, Belgian ceramists have been able to use clay with open minds so that a new kind of tradition in sculptural work has evolved over the past fifty years or more. But they have had to fight extremely hard to gain recognition and to establish their rightful position in Belgian art.

OPPOSITE: 'Hoodman'. White earthenware body mixed with grog. Heavy brown-grey engobes on 'woven' parts. $32\frac{1}{4} \times 18\frac{1}{8} \times 8\frac{1}{4}$in ($82 \times 46 \times 21$cm). White, semi-matt glaze in seven oxidised firings between $1020°$ and $1060°$C. By CARMEN DIONYSE (Belgium), 1981.

'Great Priest'. Slab-built stoneware inlaid with slip and oxides. Height 18in(45.7cm) approx. Fired to $1240°$C. By ANTOINE DE VINCK (Belgium), 1981.

'Seated Woman'. Slab-built stoneware with oxides in texture. Height 31⅞in(81cm), width 18⅞in(48cm), depth 13¾in(35cm). Reduction fired in gas kiln to 1280°C. By ANTOINE RICHARD CRÜL (Belgium), 1976.

Antoine Richard Crül, also from Belgium, continues in this tradition but his figures often grow in an unpremeditated way. He sometimes begins a piece by working directly in clay with no particular idea in mind. As the form emerges, his interest quickens, and ideas develop substance endowed with meaning. Working like this allows his sub-conscious mind more freedom to draw upon a vast store of sensations affecting the final image.

Antoine Crül does not confine his artistic activities to clay but also works through drawing, painting and etching. He sometimes sketches shapes, prompted by fantasy, side by side, until he discovers a form which

ABOVE: 'Wounded'. Slab-built stoneware, with slip and oxide colours. Height 12⅝in(32cm), width 29½in(75cm). Reduction fired in gas kiln to 1280°C. By ANTOINE RICHARD CRÜL (Belgium), 1980.

'Waiting'. Hand-built sculpture in fireclay. Height: 4ft 11 1/16 in(150cm). Fired to cone 14. By ANNA ZAMORSKA (Poland), 1981.

appeals to him. He will then re-draw that form again and again as if viewed from several angles. Although such sketches may become the starting-point for ceramic sculpture he puts them aside, never working directly from them because to do so, he feels, would deprive the piece of its essential vitality. His work hovers between the abstract and the figurative: "Of the seen and the unseen world it is the latter which interests me most." He tries to give maximum emphasis to "spiritual ideas" while making full use of those beautiful accidental textures and lines which occur during the forming process and enhance the power of visual expression.

The human head is a subject which fascinates **Kurt Spurey** (Austria). He sees it as the nerve-centre of "non-visible personality; of abstract activities; of expressions; a window of the soul". He takes the sphere as his starting-point and exploits positive and negative elements of form and space to express symbolic and formal relationships. He regards the sphere as "an endless form we can't really comprehend; therefore it represents to me all our thoughts which can break through our limitations in time and space".

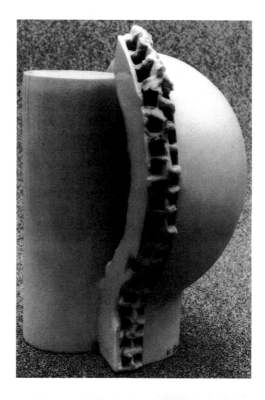

'Head'. Slip-cast porcelain construction with transparent glaze. Height 10¼in(26cm). By KURT SPUREY (Austria), 1981.

BELOW: 'Head'. Slip-cast porcelain construction based on a sphere. By KURT SPUREY (Austria), 1979.

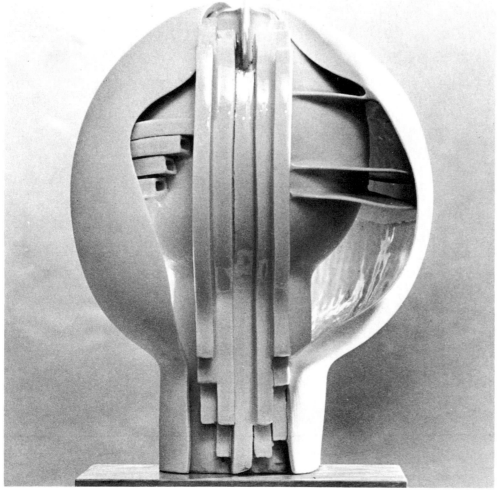

More recognisable colloquial images are created by **Gillian Still** (UK). She responds to the stimuli of an instant moment "like a snapshot". She has been influenced in the past by Han and T'ang ceramics and by the sculpture of Rosso, Manzù and Degas, but her more recent work, she feels, may owe rather more to Hogarth, Charles Keene and Daumier. There is also a surrealistic element in many of her pieces, "a touch of Hieronymus Bosch, perhaps". Incongruity and the "humour of surprise" are of constant interest and she admits that a trace of cynicism is occasionally reflected in her work. Visual humour is quickly communicated and easily understood. It is an aspect of human experience which provides enormous scope for modelled figures and animals to caricature or poke mild fun at our social relationships, situations and foibles.

'Vogue Girl'. Porcelain. 18 × 18in (45.7 × 45.7cm). By GILLIAN STILL (UK), 1980.

'Singer in a Boob Tube'. Porcelain with impressed lace decoration. Height 10in(25.4cm). By GILLIAN STILL (UK), 1981.

Among those who have developed a strong personal style in humorous ceramics of this kind are several artists whose sharp wit, clear vision and skilful manipulation of clay enable them to produce pieces offering more than just amusement. **Hilary Brock** (UK) describes himself as "basically an illustrator with a tendency to trivialise". He has little sympathy for what he calls the current penchant for intellectual content in the crafts. His interest has always been in the human figure (he remembers modelling soldiers in Plasticine at the age of five), and any background additions to these are largely regarded as 'props'. He began making his distinctive stoneware figures in the early 1970s. These were usually Victorian or Edwardian in character partly because he has an illustrator's fascination with costume (and long dresses reduced modelling difficulties) and partly because "it was easier to make pieces with the relationships I wished to show by distancing them to the period of the *Belle Epoque*". He felt that a more contemporary setting would date too quickly unless the figures were barely detailed.

An educational psychologist once described his predominantly female figures as "floozies", and these characterisations appear in an apparently endless variety of situations. "But these figures neither reflect my lifestyle nor even a fantasy world." His ideas are constantly nourished by old films and postcards.

'Tiger Hunt'. Stoneware and porcelain, hand-modelled, with on-glaze painting. Height 14in(35.6cm). By HILARY BROCK (UK), 1981.

RIGHT: 'Balloon'. Stoneware and porcelain, hand-modelled, with on-glaze painting. Height 14in(35.6cm). By HILARY BROCK (UK), 1981.

'Blind Date'. Coloured porcelain, part-glazed. 10 × 4 × 6in(25.4 × 10.2 × 15.2cm). By MONA BROOKS
(USA), 1981.

MONA BROOKS (USA) working on her
'Motorcar' with coloured porcelain, 1980.

'Motorcar'. Coloured porcelain with lustre. 11 × 9in(28 × 22.9cm). By MONA
BROOKS (USA), 1980.

Mona Brooks (USA) considers herself to be primarily a painter, although much of her recent work has been in porcelain. She feels that we "need to laugh; to see the humour in what we are doing". To achieve this end, she often portrays people as animals, or vice versa, in readily identifiable relationships. Much more powerful, often satirical, and always keenly observed humorous content can be found in the work of Jill Crowley (UK). Her 'portraits' of old men, in particular, express with more eloquence than words the ravages of life's experiences and the effects of time. Distortion, exaggeration and unrelenting attention to relevant (not fussy) detail make these pieces vital and alive.

ABOVE: 'Man in a Striped Tie'. Hand-built stoneware painted with slips, underglazes and glazes. $19\frac{11}{16} \times 9\frac{13}{16} \times 11$in ($50 \times 25 \times 28$cm). Oxidised firing to 1250°C. By JILL CROWLEY (UK), 1980.

'Man in a Blue Shirt' (detail). Hand-built stoneware, oxidised firing to 1250°C. Height $11\frac{13}{16}$in(30cm). By JILL CROWLEY (UK), 1979.

'The Smoker' (detail). Hand-built stoneware. $7\frac{7}{8}$in(20cm). By FINN HALD (Norway), 1981.

BELOW: 'Lady'. Hand-built stoneware with chrome, iron, cobalt and rutile. Height $31\frac{1}{2}$in(80cm). Fired in reduction to 1320°C in a gas kiln. By DAGNY HALD (Norway), 1981.

Finn and Dagny Hald (Norway) model figures which are placed in almost surreal situations. Their work is individually titled and often tinged with ironic humour.

'Thoughtful Jockey'. Hand-built stoneware. $7\frac{7}{8}$in(20cm). By FINN HALD (Norway), 1981.

'Bathers'. White earthenware, slab-built, sprayed and painted with underglaze colours and ceramic pencil. Width 15in(38.1cm). Oxidised firing to 1080°C. By RUTH FRANKLIN (UK), 1980.

Drawing, rather than modelling, is used by **Ruth Franklin** (UK) to interpret her impressions of people and environments in humorous vein. "For as long as I can remember I have been drawing people; characters and situations that intrigue and amuse me. I go to Cruft's Dog Show each year to sketch the eccentric people with their eccentric dogs. I draw on the train, in pubs, cafés, parks. I started drawing these characters on thrown pots, cutting out rims to form the outlines of buildings, signs, doors, backgrounds to accompany the drawings." Moving into slab-building, it seemed natural that the outline of her drawing should become the shape of the clay, and her recent work has evolved in this way. Her pieces remain ceramic in that the clay slabs are fired to 1120°C, but emulsion paints and oil-based colours are preferred to glazes. "Since my work is more sculptural I no longer feel the need to use glazes."

Porcelain pot, thrown, turned and cut when leather-hard. Ceramic pencil and underglaze colours under a clear, matt glaze sprayed very thinly. Height 12in(30.5cm). Oxidised firing to 1260°C. By RUTH FRANKLIN (UK), 1980.

'R.O. Series VII' (incline). Slab construction in 'T' material, with lead carbonate and barium glaze over manganese dioxide brushwork and cobalt lettering, fired to cone 08 (after initial bisque firing to cone 8 before colour is applied). $11\frac{13}{16} \times 11\frac{7}{16}$in($30 \times 29$cm). By JOHN TESCHENDORFF (Australia), 1979.

The use of paints and other non-ceramic materials is not uncommon among sculptors who choose to work in clay. **John Teschendorff** (Australia) introduces "wood, metal, cloth, acrylic, found objects, literally anything that satisfies the imagery". His early pieces caused a furore ("not ceramics you know!") although in all other respects he uses traditional ceramic techniques.

Another Australian ceramist, **Vincent McGrath,** chooses to remain totally within tradition so far as methods and techniques are concerned, but his approach to image-making is equally uninhibited. His association with contemporary American West Coast Bay artists, coupled with a respect for the Abstract Expressionist movement in ceramics, totally altered his thinking towards clay. Working on a large scale and

allowing "the formal qualities of design to be overtaken by the inherent expressionistic qualities of the material", he explores a "passionate response to the harsh climate of the northern Australian landscape". He uses a raku-type body covered with a white slip for his large, flat or slightly concave pieces. Firing once to 1100°C, he has developed a range of brightly coloured slips and stains to project "a kind of timelessness associated with a desert landscape" through the interplay of semi-descriptive forms and abstract images which tend to float across and out of the picture plane.

RIGHT: 'Victoria River Downs'. Earthenware with clay slips (50 parts talc; 50 parts ball clay) and underglaze stains, oxides and low-fire glazes. $26\frac{3}{8} \times 25\frac{9}{16}$in ($67 \times 65$cm). By VINCENT MCGRATH (Australia), 1981.

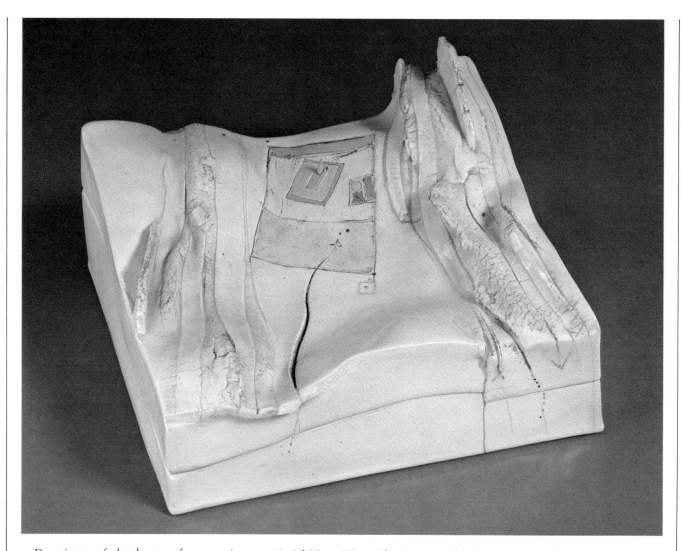

Drawings of landscape from various viewpoints "and the kinds of space we find ourselves confronted with (real and illusory)" also occupy **Paula Winokur** (USA). "An aerial perspective has become the most challenging for me to explore, along with the idea of hidden places, treasure maps and specific 'sites'. The small ceramic 'drawings' are places extracted from a larger area. They are, to me, like short lines of poetry (a haiku, perhaps) where I can focus attention on a particular object or shape or collection of shapes that contain some special significance." She has concentrated over the past few years on 'box' forms in porcelain. This material, she feels, is of an intimate nature, "it does not allow for grand scale, but wants to remain within the bounds of personal contact". The transformation of clay from one state to another is for her almost "magical", while the box form itself "inviting an opening, presents a challenge to create a mystery for what is inside".

'Aerial View: Winter Plowing'. Porcelain box with clear glaze, sulphates, stains and lustres. 13 × 12 × 7in(33 × 30.5 × 17.8cm). Reduction fired to cone 10. By PAULA WINOKUR (USA), 1979.

Linear drawing as a means of decorating ceramic surfaces is one of the oldest and most direct forms of treatment. **Siddig El' Nigoumi** (UK) was born in the Sudan where the cultures of Africa and Islam merge. He grew up among a people who used a variety of burnished, unglazed pots and also vessels made out of calabash with shiny surfaces, sometimes decorated with intricate incised linear patterns. He studied, and has taught, in England for several years, but the inspiration for his work still comes from the Middle East, particularly Arabic calligraphy and floral patterns found on brass and other metal utensils in that part of the world. Each design is carefully drawn out on paper before he commences work on the burnished surface of his pots, but it is not uncommon for him to sit "for quite a while" with a dish in front of him and "let it dictate what suits it for decoration. Sometimes I hear myself asking it what it wants and then wait for the answer".

Earthenware dish, press-moulded, burnished and smoked, with incised design, coloured black and red, fired to 800°C in an electric kiln. 14 × 11in (35.6 × 28cm). By SIDDIG EL'NIGOUMI (UK), 1981.

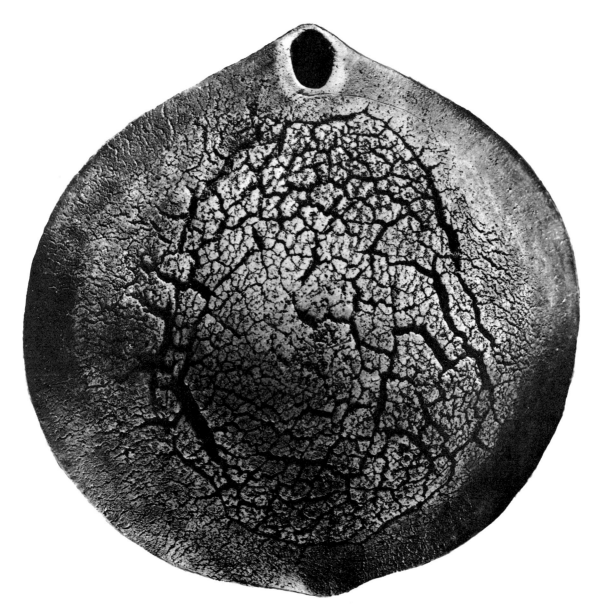

Taking one's references from outside one's immediate experience of time, place and circumstance, without understanding the complex network making up the culture which produced them, can lead to work which is no more than pale imitation, lacking soul.

Bernard Leach directed Western potters to look towards the East for example and inspiration, but many have done so without the benefit of his knowledge and inner conviction. Consequently, superficial works, paying lip service to the Oriental aesthetic, far outnumber those which successfully survive the transition. The work of Bernard's son, **David Leach**, continues within what has become known as the Leach tradition, with forms and glazes that can be traced to China, Japan and Korea. But a

porcelain bowl by him or even a teapot has its own unmistakable identity related to, but not copied from, Oriental pieces. His concern for fine craftsmanship and technical perfection, together with a natural feeling for the material ensure that each piece is recognisably from his hand.

Len Castle (New Zealand), who worked with Bernard Leach and **Shoji Hamada** for a period, says that it was Leach who set him thinking, developing attitudes, and who acted as the catalyst in crystallising his own personal philosophy. Hamada also contributed by demonstrating an earthy robustness, strength of form, and the importance of grasping moments of intuitive awareness: of feeling, thinking and acting in equal balance. Len Castle makes pots to fulfil functional requirements; to meet his own

Hanging, flattened, stoneware vase. $14\frac{3}{16} \times 14\frac{3}{16}$in($36 \times 36$cm). Stretched slab construction surface washed with yellow ochre. Oxidation/reduction firing to $1280°–1300°$C in an oil-fuelled kiln. By LEN CASTLE (New Zealand), 1969.

psychological needs; to express his attitudes; to wrestle with the problems of form; for the elation he gains from discovering the unknown; and for the passionate involvement with clay, a substance for which he has "respect and love".

Peter Stichbury (New Zealand) is another potter who, having worked with Leach and **Michael Cardew** in Nigeria, reflects some-thing of their influence in his work. He likes "skilful pots made expressively" but does not enjoy "clumsy work which passes for expressive work". He makes pots to please himself first and foremost, because he feels this to be essential if he is to maintain standards and directions while continuing to develop as an individual. "In pleasing myself, hopefully, I will please others also."

Two jars with screw stoppers, stoneware. Rear piece with barium matt glaze, base and panels unglazed but pot pre-dipped in ochre wash. Panels textured with Nigerian potter's roulette (Kwali potters). Heights $18\frac{1}{8}$in(46cm) and $14\frac{3}{16}$in(36cm). Front piece has two glazes, Tessha over barium matt and wax-resist brushwork. Both are fired to Orton cone 10 in an LPG kiln. By PETER STICHBURY (New Zealand), 1981.

Islamic art has also proved a useful reference point for potters working within a European tradition. **Alan Caiger-Smith** (UK) and **Alan Peascod** (Australia) are two of these, but while Caiger-Smith's interest in this respect is concentrated upon fluent brushwork and lustre decoration reminiscent of that to be seen on Hispano-Moresque wares, Peascod's pieces appear to owe more to the vessel forms of the Middle East, where he has worked intermittently for several years. Although Alan Caiger-Smith is conscious of the influences upon his work, he has never attempted any direct derivations: "It is rather that I am aware, as it were, of playing an instrument which was used by them (Islamic potters), though the tunes and variations are different."

Jar on tripod, stoneware with matt glaze. Height of jar 13¾in(35cm). Fired to 1280°C. By ALAN PEASCOD (**Australia**), 1981.

OPPOSITE: Bowl, earthenware, with calligraphic brushwork in blue (cobalt and copper) on white tin glaze containing whiting (hence the speckling of the painted area). Re-firing in a lustre kiln at low temperature has partially reduced the copper. Width 11in(28cm), depth 3in(7.6cm). By ALAN CAIGER-SMITH (UK), 1980.

ABOVE: 'Abstract Forms'. Stoneware, with turquoise glaze. Oxidised. Heights 14in(35.6cm) and 7in(17.8cm). By VAL BARRY (UK), 1981.

The ease with which people can travel from one continent to another has encouraged the rapid assimilation of ideas and influences powerful enough to affect, and possibly re-direct, the work of many potters. **Val Barry's** (UK) visit to China, for example, inspired her to create slab-built forms derived from Chinese junks. **Karin Hessenberg** (UK) began making thick, carved porcelain objects following her return from a year spent travelling in South America, where she had been deeply impressed by Inca stone carvings in Peru. She wished to combine "a carved, sculptural appearance with fineness"; this initial work gave rise to the development of her cut and overlapped pieces in smoked porcelain.

LEFT: Smoked porcelain pot, thrown, cut and re-shaped. Height 6in(15.2cm). Low fired to 950°–980°C in an electric kiln, followed by sawdust firing. By KARIN HESSENBERG (UK), 1982. In the author's collection.

Harlan House (Canada) believes that with so few ceramic traditions behind them, most Canadians "adopt someone else's". He much admires, and looks towards, Oriental ceramics and also the work of early European potters. But, as in most countries where the kind of studio ceramics described in this book are popular, one can do no more than generalise about national characteristics or style in Canadian work. Clearly the proximity of the United States of America has influenced many ceramists working in a sculptural vein, although there seems to be a slightly more reserved, less competitive feeling about it.

The emphasis upon 'art' ceramics in American universities has produced many people whose approach to clay is utterly uninhibited and, in a way, rarely paralleled elsewhere. **Erik Gronborg** (USA) is one of these. He says that his training allowed him to make a conscious decision to choose ceramics as his personal vehicle for artistic expression. He believes that "ceramics is art and it will be accepted as art when the maker creates it as art". The important difference between the 'potter' and the ceramic artist, he believes, is that to the potter, the plate, the teapot and the cup indicate the *function* of the work while, to the artist, these are the *subjects* of the work in the same way that landscape can be the subject for a painting.

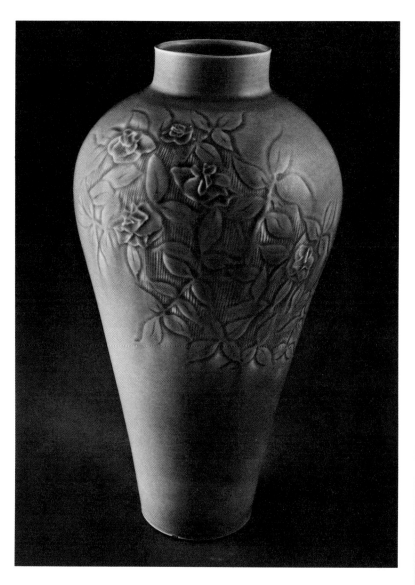

Porcelain vase, thrown and carved with wild rose design under pale green celadon glaze. Height 14in(35.5cm). By HARLAN HOUSE (Canada), 1982.

Cup, black basalt, hand-built, with stamped decoration, fired to cone 6. Height 4½in(11.4cm). By ERIK GRONBORG (USA).

3 CERAMIC FORM

The potter, perhaps more than any other craftsman, has to deal with so many variables arising in the process of making that his chosen materials and methods must be fully understood if he is to reach a point where technical aspects no longer dominate aesthetic considerations.

For example, work executed in a coarse, granular clay used for raku or heavily grogged stoneware demands a different approach to that carried out in a smooth porcelain body. One clay may require a bold, vigorous treatment while another will be more amenable to the precise and gentle touch.

Irrespective of which method, or combination of methods, are used in giving form to ideas, the potter must work in sympathy with his clay at every stage. Apart from prerequisites of function (if any), he is free to exercise his art in whatever way seems appropriate to him. There can be no room for dogma in ceramics any more than in other forms of art. There will always be those who seek to lay down rules concerning techniques or aesthetic criteria but, in truth, there can only be personal preferences, which are themselves subject to modification and change. Even a consensus does not justify a dictum since what is accepted as a rule, norm or ideal today may be broken, disproved or rejected tomorrow. But the pursuit of novelty *at all costs* usually gives birth to superficial work at any level and will be recognized as such. On the other hand, a genuine expression of feeling, of response to an idea, an experience or, perhaps, to the potential of the ceramic medium itself is more likely to be communicated through the work.

Clay bodies (as they are called) are often made up of several clays or compounded from one or more clays to which other ingredients are added in order to adjust the colour, texture, plasticity or maturing tem-

Hand-built stoneware jug with drawn and painted decoration, fired in oxidation. Height 12$\frac{3}{16}$in(31cm). By ALISON BRITTON (UK), 1979. In the Crafts Council Collection.

perature. The three broad categories of earthenware (up to 1200°C), stoneware (over 1200°C), and porcelain, are all extensively used by studio potters, but clays designed for a particular temperature or purpose may be employed outside their intended range to give certain qualities to a ceramic piece.

Earthenware bodies, coloured from off-white to dark reddish-brown when fired, normally remain porous unless glazed. Slip-decorated and tin-glazed wares of different kinds made from such clays have been popular for domestic studio pottery over

OPPOSITE: 'Iris' vase. Porcelain, slip-cast form with hand-built iris, carved and excised, chrome oxide brushwork, once fired (cone 10). Height 18in(45.2cm). By HARLAN HOUSE (Canada), 1982.

many years. Recently, earthenware has enjoyed something of a revival for its capacity to display a wide range of bright colours. In part, this is a reaction to a market which had become saturated with rather drab, unremarkable stonewares.

The drama and immediacy of raku firing has also attracted a strong following and encouraged experiments with other low-fired wares, where much of the visual interest is contributed by the firing process itself. Firing is conducted well below the usual temperatures for earthenware. Open, coarse-textured bodies are necessary if pieces are to survive the thermal shock to which they are subjected in raku. This granular material is best when worked freely and spontaneously. Technical equipment required for raku is minimal and the process offers considerable scope for creative work. Traditionally, raku pots are relatively small but an increasing number of potters who have turned to this technique are now making large pieces in excess of 2 ft (60 cm) high.

Stoneware possesses a strength and durability unmatched by lower fired wares. Many clay bodies are multipurpose in the sense that they may be used for both low and high-temperature firing. At the top temperatures, the clay particles fuse into a dense, usually impervious, mass. The colours tend to be more muted in stoneware glazes. There is a closer unison of body and glaze, and greater interaction between them, producing visual qualities which can only be partially simulated in earthenwares.

The greatest impact since the early 1970s has probably been made in the field of studio porcelain. Porcelain is a material long regarded as difficult to work with but capable of the utmost refinement. While porcelain was not exactly uncommon among studio ceramics, it is only in the last decade that the world-wide explosion of interest has occurred. The smoothness, purity and translucency of porcelain retains its timeless appeal, and its white body allows colours to remain clean and fresh. Most pieces made in porcelain are on an intimate scale. They invite close inspection and handling to be fully appreciated and enjoyed. Bone china, which is itself a kind of porcelain, is rarely used as a plastic body but it has found favour with several potters who slip-cast pieces for ultimate carving or painting.

Porcelain bowl, wheel-thrown and altered. Height 9in(22.9cm). Small amounts of silicon carbide powder have been added to the porcelain body so that gases formed during firing bubble through the matt glaze. Reduction fired to Orton cone 11. By SALLY BOWEN PRANGE (USA), 1981.

Throwing and turning

Throwing is the forming method most people tend to associate with pot-making. Apart from slip-casting, it is the quickest method, and certainly the most dramatic to watch. A skilled thrower acquires a fluency where he is as one with his wheel and clay. The pressure of his hands, the amount of water needed for efficient lubrication, and the speed of the revolving wheel-head are adjusted to suit the character of the clay body and the form as it develops. It requires understanding, control and, above all, sensitivity towards all these factors if the piece is to have truly expressive quality.

Some potters add a generous proportion of granular material, such as sand or grog, to give the body extra 'tooth' and texture. This also has the effect of providing stiffening support to large, wide or tall forms which might otherwise collapse before the throwing movement is completed. As might be expected, such clays respond well to vigorous treatment where no attempt is made to disguise the marks of the forming process.

Porcelain, on the other hand, is creamily smooth and even. It requires more delicate guidance. The porcelain potter must beware wetting the clay too much. Equally, he must prevent the loss of surface lubrication, which can happen quite suddenly with this body, or it may snag and stick to his hand with consequent distortion or collapse.

The speed with which clay can be shaped on the wheel has made this method an obvious choice for production potters. Repetition throwing demands skill and discipline of a different order from random 'one-off' pieces. A steady rhythmic pattern of work is necessary for consistency and economy.

John Dermer (Australia) is a production potter who also finds time to make individual pieces. Ninety per cent of his output is tableware. Since these pieces are intended for everyday use, he stresses the importance of functional design and high-quality finish. There is no excuse for rough bottoms on pots likely to be pushed across table-tops.

Unfortunately, the 'natural' rustic image of hand-thrown stonewares is too often the excuse for poor finishing practice which negates much of its appeal in use.

Salt-glazed pot with colour variations from pale to amber, through orange and green to blue-black. Height 6¾in(17.2cm). By JOHN DERMER (**Australia**), 1981. In the author's collection.

ABOVE: JEFF MINCHAM (**Australia**) throwing a large 'planter', 1982.

Like John Dermer in his concern for sound functional design, **Gwyn Pigott** (Australia) makes a range of fine tablewares. Working mainly in porcelain with two basic glazes, her pieces are beautifully thrown and turned with a sharp clarity of form and superb finish.

The circular section imposed by the wheel can be altered by pressure from within or without before the thrown pot has dried out. It is possible to re-dampen surfaces for manipulation at the bone-dry stage but this tends to pose additional problems. Cylinders can be made oval in section by removing the base, or making an elliptical slit in it, and gently coaxing the clay with even pressure from opposing sides. Or, it may be paddled and beaten to create a squared or other section. The clay can be faceted with a taut wire or sharp knife. It can be cut and overlapped or sliced and rejoined.

ABOVE: Dinner set in 'insulator' porcelain body, translucent where thin, gas kiln reduction firing. Diameter of dinner plate $9\frac{13}{16}$in(25cm). This potter is perhaps best remembered in Britain as Gwyn Hansen. These pieces were made when she was resident at The Jam Factory workshops in Adelaide. By GWYN PIGOTT (**Australia**), 1980.

Porcelain teapot with cane handle and beige-pink glaze, reduction fired. Height $6\frac{11}{16}$in(17cm). By GWYN PIGOTT (**Australia**), 1981.

'Zin Zang'. Thrown and altered earthenware, multi-fired with various glazes maturing at temperatures between cones 06 and 09. 13 × 12 × 11in(33 × 30.5 × 28cm). By HARVEY GOLDMAN (USA), 1982. Courtesy of Impressions Gallery, Boston.

Greg Daly (Australia) throws his larger pieces in two parts in order not to overwork the clay at this stage. The simple bulbous shape of the thrown pot rising from a relatively small base is worked upon immediately while the clay is still wet from the wheel. Pressure is applied from within to stretch and expand the clay outwards. The shaping and refining of these forms may take up to four or five days to complete as they stiffen. Consequently, the walls of pieces 30in high may become quite thin in places ($\frac{1}{8}$in.) where it has been stretched. Dry glazes are carefully chosen and sprayed in a manner that gives variable but controlled thickness, and emphasizes the undulating surface. He tries to express energy and movement in each of these forms. To produce the initial pots by hand-building methods would be a shade tedious and without the immediacy, flexibility and physical strength of the thrown form.

Stoneware form, thrown initially and then altered and expanded by internal pressure, sprayed with terracotta, titanium and iron oxide. Height 26in(66cm). Fired with gas in reduction to 1300°C. By GREG DALY (Australia), 1981.

An unusual technique is used by **Josef Szirer** (Australia) to give his thrown pots a different coloured surface from the body underneath. A lump of white stoneware clay is centred on the wheel and a sleeve of darker clay, previously thrown, is slid over this. Centreing is then completed and the clay is opened and pulled up into a tall narrow cylinder. Decoration is incised into the cylinder through the darker clay with a needle. Throwing is then continued to stretch the cylinder outwards into a fatter form. The outer sleeve of clay cracks, revealing the lighter body underneath in a 'natural' way. Bright barium glazes gain textural variety when applied to pots produced by this method.

Stoneware vase, made in white stoneware over which a darker clay 'sleeve' is fitted at an early stage of throwing, so that the outer layer is stretched and cracks to show the lighter body underneath. Incised decoration, with barium glaze. Height 17in(43.2cm) approx. By JOSEF SZIRER (Australia), 1981.

The process of throwing plastic clay is immensely satisfying. Where economy of labour and materials is an important factor, such as in a production workshop making tableware, pieces can be thrown efficiently enough to require little further 'finishing' after removal from the wheel. Certain shapes, however, require to be thrown with thick walls, followed by precise turning when leather-hard. It would be quite impossible to achieve the complex contours of **Geoffrey Swindell's** (UK) porcelain forms by throwing alone. **Glenn Doell's** (USA) deeply carved porcelain bowls are carefully thrown with variable wall thickness. In some cases the carved sections are $1-1\frac{1}{2}$ in. thick. These pieces are thrown from about 70 lb. of porcelain with sufficient judgement to leave a fairly uniform wall thickness after completion of the carved areas. His working method overall "is extremely slow. The clay is well-aged (in some cases a year or more), wedged so *no* air bubbles are remaining, thrown and dried for at least one or two months. Only in the bone-dry state is carving begun. Handling the piece at the leather-hard stage produces cracks which show up only after the final firing".

Porcelain pot, thrown and turned, white and green (copper) with purple crackle lines (from thinly applied gold lustre). Height $4\frac{1}{2}$in(11.4cm). Fired in oxidation. By GEOFFREY SWINDELL (UK), 1980.

'Coquette'. Thrown and deeply carved porcelain, unglazed. Height 10in(25.4cm), diameter 14in(35.1cm). By GLENN DOELL (USA), 1981.

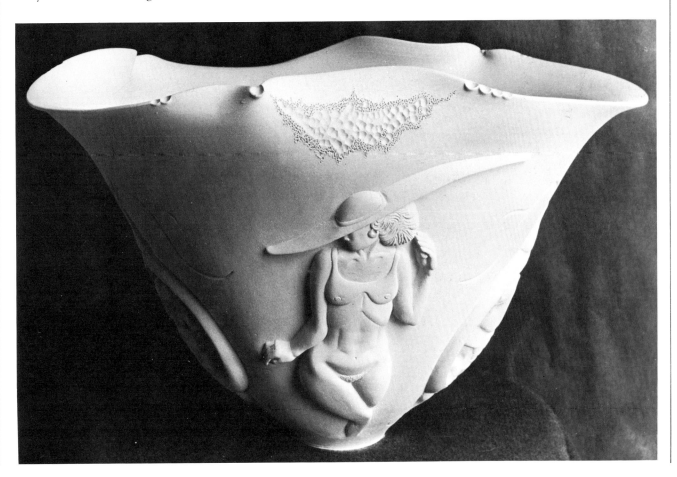

Column vases, porcelain, thrown and assembled from sections on the wheel. Heights 26in(66.1cm) to 29in(73.2cm). By CATHERINE HIERSOUX (USA), 1982.

While some potters feel that greater fluency can be gained from throwing and completing a form in one piece, others prefer to build up large pieces from several sections luted together with slip and re-thrown to smooth over the joins and refine the profile. **Lucie Rie's** (UK) distinctive bottle vases often have a well-defined foot, rounded belly, sloping shoulder, tall neck and wide-flaring lip. The flowing profile is given subtle emphasis by throwing foot, belly and neck separately, and gently squeezing the neck into a slightly oval cross-section at the junction with the shoulder of the pot while the clay is still plastic. This action distorts the lip away from the severely horizontal so that it becomes an undulating curve in total harmony with the form from which it grows. The techniques used in her work are demanding in that the forming process, surface decoration and glazing are all completed in the raw state before the brittle clay object is committed to the kiln. Over the past thirty years or so, all her work has been produced by this method and once fired to 1250°C in an electric kiln.

The tall porcelain columns of **Catherine Hiersoux** (USA) are constructed from a series of loosely thrown cylinders. The base cylinder is allowed to stiffen before she adds

OPPOSITE: Bottle in stoneware with pink, green and grey spirals. Height 15in(38cm). By LUCIE RIE (UK), 1979.

Column vases, stoneware, thrown in two sections, joined and turned. Height of taller vase $19\frac{11}{16}$in(50cm). The decoration consists of changes of tone and texture relating to a fairly simple form. A band is placed at the point where the form changes direction. The band itself consists of rich orange-coloured exposed body and black slip, in addition to the turned 'mouldings'. The shiny tenmoku glaze at the top contrasts with the matt brown of brushed slip on the bottom section. By WEST MARSHALL (UK), 1979.

the next section, which is rethrown on the base, and so on until the final height is reached. All her work "comes out of historical traditions and much from classical origins. Though none of the pieces are created with a conscious attempt to copy or remake classical pieces, I work with forms as they develop on the wheel, generally through many series. The attempt is towards evoking concepts of elegance, clarity,

lyricism and ideal form".

I watched some very large thrown stoneware pots being made by Australian potters during a ceramics conference in Sydney in 1981. Sections were stiffened rapidly with the aid of a large-nozzled blow torch flame which was played over the wet clay as it rotated slowly on a wheel-head. Enormous pots were quickly built up by accelerating the drying process in this way.

Pedestal bowl, thrown and turned stoneware, 'T' material basalt body, fired to 1290°C followed by airbrushed bronze lustre fired to 750°C (around rim). Height and diameter both 4¾in(12.1cm). By GLYN HUGO (UK), 1982.

Pedestal bowl, thrown and turned porcelain, fired to 1290°C in reduction followed by brushing with gold and copper lustre and re-fired to 750°C. Height 5¼in(13.4cm). By GLYN HUGO (UK).

Hand-building

The more innovative and imaginative building techniques have been developed by those ceramists whose work is produced without the aid of the potter's wheel except to contribute parts to the whole. Adapting materials and methods to resolve ideas and achieve specific aims has resulted in some intriguing individual approaches. Clay rolled out into sheets or slabs of any thickness from less than $\frac{1}{16}$ in. up to $2\frac{1}{2}$ in. can be used for various forming and decorative

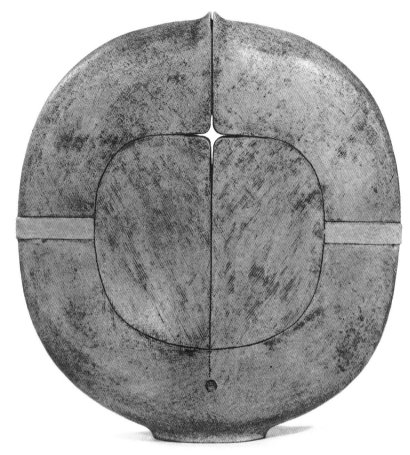

'Closed Form'. Stoneware, coil-built, sgraffito with iron in ash glaze (some parts have cobalt feldspathic glaze) fired to 1220°C in oxidation. Height $10\frac{5}{8}$in(27cm). By HANS DE JONG (Holland), 1980.

BELOW: 'Round Vessels'. Stoneware, ash and feldspar glaze fired to 1340°C in oxidation. Heights $9\frac{13}{16}$in(25cm) to $11\frac{13}{16}$in(30cm). By DIETER CRUMBIEGEL (West Germany), 1978.

purposes. Some of these latter processes are described in Chapter 4.

One of the most common methods of building with slabs is to use them in the leather-hard state when they can be freely handled without risk of distortion. Angular, flat-sided forms like those by **Antje Bruggemann-Breckwoldt** (Germany), **Dieter Crumbiegel** (Germany) and **Otto Natzler** (USA) offer considerable scope for geometric division or to display coloured and textured glaze surfaces.

Oval form with three openings and oval base, stoneware, slab construction, ivory celadon glaze with melt fissures, skinning and fire marks, reduction fired. Height 8¾in(22.2cm). By OTTO NATZLER (USA), 1980.

BELOW: Relief wall sculpture in two parts, stoneware with ash and feldspar glaze containing iron, fired to 1340°C in oxidation. 3ft 10⁷⁄₁₆in(118 × 32cm). By DIETER CRUMBIEGEL (West Germany), 1981.

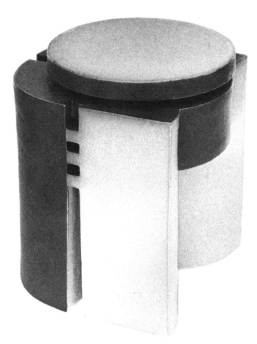

ABOVE: 'Walzenform'. Stoneware sculpture, thrown and assembled, with matt black glaze in parts. Fired to 1300°C. $8\frac{5}{8} \times 7\frac{1}{2}$in(22 × 19cm). By FRITZ VEHRING (West Germany), 1979.

Slab-built vessel with tall foot and diagonal divisions in light and dark stoneware bodies. $11 \times 7\frac{1}{16} \times 3\frac{3}{8}$in(28 × 18 × 8.5cm). Reduction fired to 1300°C. By ANTJE BRÜGGEMANN-BRECKWOLDT (West Germany), 1980.

Bottle form, stoneware, with iron-blue glazes fired in reduction to 1360°C. $10\frac{5}{8} \times 9\frac{7}{16} \times 2\frac{3}{4}$in (27 × 24 × 7cm). By KARL SCHEID (West Germany), 1981.

ERIK GRONBORG (USA) applying photographic decals to a plate form.

Antje Bruggemann-Breckwoldt uses two stoneware clays, one a light grey and one a dark brown. She feels that her vases should function as such. Their monolithic presence is enhanced by the way in which she has explored her interest in sub-dividing the surface into positive geometric facets. She aims to achieve "an harmonious appearance, something like an object of meditation".

Erik Gronborg (USA) grew up in Denmark but emigrated to the USA in his twenties. He sees his porcelain work as being related to the traditions of eighteenth and nineteenth-century Europe, "with the emphasis on fragile delicacy, brilliant colours in lustres, and elaborate decoration". But his processes and imagery are very much part of the twentieth century, with a strong flavour of contemporary America. All his ceramics are hand-built from slabs in either porcelain (fired to cone 6 with a clear glaze

and re-fired several times to add the photographic decals and the lustres) or a light-coloured stoneware, usually for the larger pieces. Also, his pieces are assembled from several parts and rather than disguise the joins he emphasizes them "to give the works a strong sense of structure, of construction that will give a certain logic to the relationship of the parts". At the same time, he tries to give the work "a sense of the unique touch of the creative hand and of the special soft, plastic nature of clay". Erik Gronborg exploits this quality by allowing the clay to bend, twist, tear and fold as he works, thereby ensuring the individuality of each form.

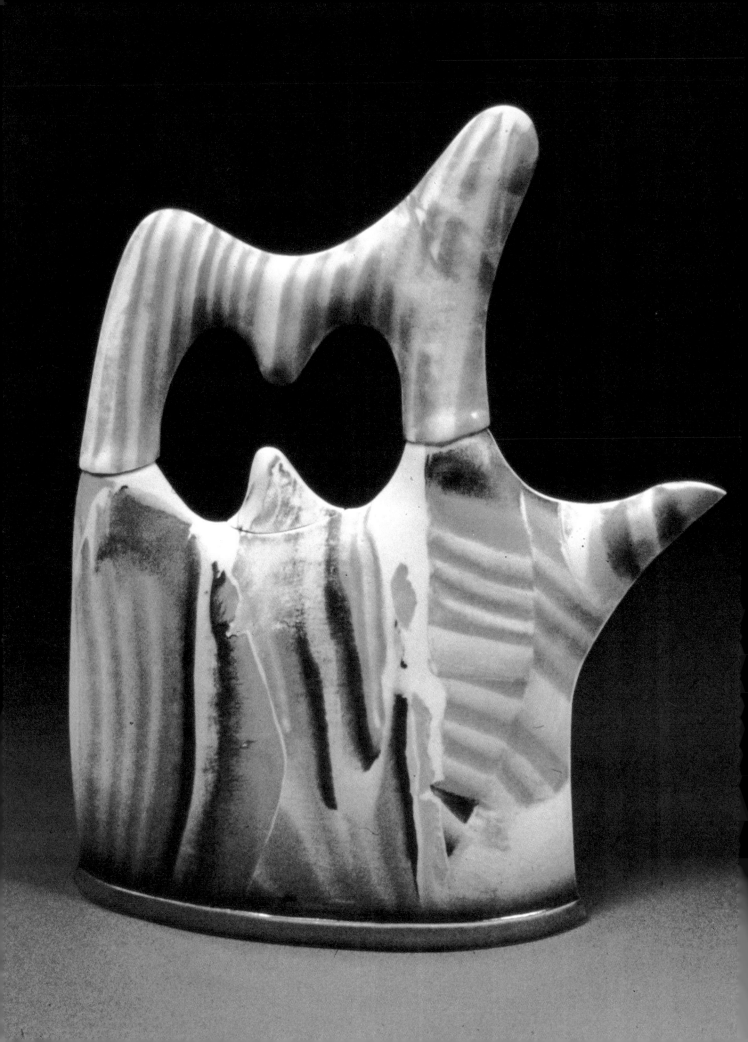

Sometimes potters convert quite ordinary forms into the extraordinary by a simple addition or subtraction to the walls of the piece. Deliberate pressure may also be used to distort the vessel, bringing unexpected variety to the profile. A multiplication of simple, basic shapes, which alone would be unremarkable, may be joined together to create a complex structure with many facets to catch light and trap shadows. The nature and condition of the chosen clay and the processes by which it is formed will be further affected by the personality and intent of the potter. His feeling for, and understanding of, his subject matter, whatever this might be, will be balanced and conditioned by sympathetic 'know-how' concerning his materials. He cannot often rely on the happy accident, although he will try to remain aware of opportunities which may offer themselves during the making process.

The standard teapot is a familiar object and most children could draw some kind of symbolic representation of it. Industrially-made European teapots of the eighteenth and nineteenth centuries were often disguised as vegetables, cottages, and so on, but to create a form for such an obvious function while relying solely on minimal decoration for aesthetic appeal remains an enjoyable challenge for many contemporary potters.

Walter Keeler's (UK) stoneware teapot has an oval base and extended handle. Its clean profile seems to owe more to soldered tin-plate cans than to traditional teapot forms, yet it is a perfectly natural use of clay. Precisely drawn indented vertical lines from shoulder to boot, and along the spout, echo the angularity of the piece. He does not consciously bring any outside influences to bear on his ideas but feels strongly aware of the long tradition of pot-making in England, particularly salt-glazed wares of the eighteenth century.

BELOW LEFT: 'Wavy-necked Bottle'. Porcelain with ash glaze over barium glaze. Height 10in(25.4cm). By GEOFFREY EASTOP (UK), 1982.

Salt-glazed teapot. Height approx 10in(25.4cm). The outside is covered with a china clay and feldspar slip which gives pale grey through gold to red colours with salt glaze. By WALTER KEELER (UK), 1980.

OPPOSITE: Porcelain teapot, hand-built with inlaid coloured clays, glaze sprayed and airbrushed. Height 16in(40.6cm). Fired in oxidation to cone 9. By KAETE BRITTIN SHAW (USA), 1981.

A rather more conventional form is used by **Tim Mather** (USA) for his porcelain teapot, but the visual interest is increased by wire-cut facets on the body wall and an unusual strap handle. The surface is mottled where the white body shines through a fluid, wood-ash glaze.

The strap handle of **Bryan Trueman's** (Australia) teapot also has additional clay crowning the arch and there is no denying the intended function of the piece. **Kaete Brittin Shaw** (USA) has started with the notion of 'teapot' to explore a series of individual pieces which she says "could be functional", but which have evolved increasingly towards the decorative. She believes that a few people have used them for tea although her concept was that they should be only semi-functional. Unlike most potters who make teapots, she slab-builds these pieces with inlaid coloured porcelain.

LEFT: Porcelain teapot, wheel-thrown, with cut facets and wood-ash glaze, fired in reduction to Orton cone 11. Height 11in(28cm). The body gleams white through the olive-green glaze. By TIM MATHER (USA), 1980

ABOVE: Stoneware teapot with rich iron glaze, reduction fired. By BRYAN TRUEMAN (Australia), 1981.

Porcelain teapot, hand-built from inlaid coloured slabs, airbrushed and sprayed, fired to cone 9 in oxidation. Height 14in(35.6cm). By KAETE BRITTIN SHAW (USA), 1981.

Teapots, made from thin slabs of fine-textured red stoneware body (with added stains in parts) fired to cone 6. By VIRGINIA CARTWRIGHT (USA), 1982.

More obviously straightforward slab construction is employed by **Philip Cornelius** (USA) for his unusual teapots, but **Virginia Cartwright** (USA) cuts and re-shapes sheets of clay to approximate more closely to the conventional teapot shape. Initially, a cylinder is made with a thin slab of red stoneware clay and then pie-shaped wedges are cut out downwards from the top edge, to allow the form to be folded inward and the cut edges to be luted together. A further slab is attached to this re-shaped cylinder top and the pot is then inverted so that similar wedge-cutting can be done at the other end of the cylinder (which now becomes the top of the final form). This treatment produces a distinctive faceted pot for which lids are carefully hand-built to fit perfectly, so that none of the work is done on the potter's wheel. For her, the character of the clay stimulates creative thought and expression.

Virginia Cartwright says that although her shapes are traditional, her approach is "playful". She believes that the visual interplay of the parts of the teapot have a human and almost humorous quality. Functional forms appeal to her because "they invite the viewer to interact with them. When the viewer holds the vessel or uses it, he communicates with the person who made it, and completes a sort of cycle. For me, a functional pot that is merely displayed, but never held or used, is an uncompleted piece". (These are feelings which are shared by many other potters.) The smooth red clay is a filter-pressed body ('Redstone', produced by Quyle Kilns, Murphys, California, USA) which she finds "responds with the sensitivity of porcelain, but does not have its negative characteristics of warping and cracking". It retains a similar appearance to its leather-hard state when fired but left unglazed.

'Baker'. Porcelain teapot, unglazed, made from very thin sheets of clay. Height 9 × 8 × 3in (22.9 × 20.3 × 7.7cm). By PHILIP CORNELIUS (USA), 1981.

Teapot, made from thin slabs of fine-textured red stoneware body fired to cone 6. By VIRGINIA CARTWRIGHT (USA), 1982.

Three porcelain vases, ('Container series'), made from thin slabs, combed decoration washed with cobalt sulphate under a transparent glaze. By NINA GABY (USA), 1982.

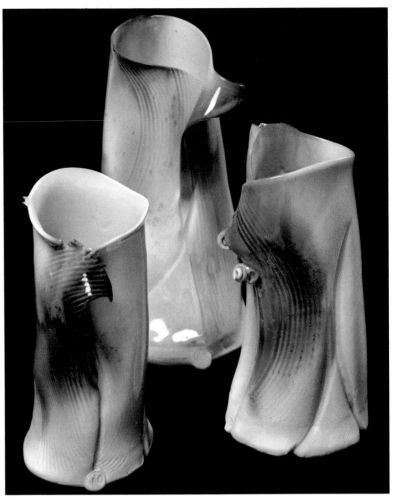

Wall-mounted 'Shelf Piece'. Buff earthenware body with white slips and glazed fired to 1150°C. The two ceramic forms are set on a shelf against a matt white textured background. By GORDON BALDWIN (UK), 1982.

ABOVE: Hand-built porcelain tea set with zinc crystalline glaze fired in oxidation to cone 10. Height of teapot 11in(28cm), length of tray 12in(30,5cm). By NINA GABY (USA), 1982.

Striped, marbled dish (alternating stoneware and porcelain bodies) with shino glaze. Diameter $12\frac{1}{16}$in(31cm). Oxidised to 1260°C. By EWEN HENDERSON (UK), 1980.

Joining coils, slabs, strips and patches of clay together to build a form allows more time for reflection, and opportunities to adjust and adapt to the work as it grows. Such pieces often acquire a 'depth', an unpredictability of form or surface, quite different from anything produced solely on the wheel. **Ewen Henderson** (UK) makes pots which are almost impossible to categorise. They do not conform to any idealistic notion of profile and proportion. Although they may be considered vessel forms, they are assemblages of different clay bodies (stoneware, porcelain, bone china), some clear, some stained with oxides and body colour, pieced together in various ways so that pots and decoration are one and the same. Ewen Henderson's motifs include spirals, stripes, radial movements and laminated effects resulting in a richly expressive surface. He finds that the most difficult part of the work lies in relating the decorative treatment to the form or, alternatively, "in arriving at a form organically related to the decoration".

A mixture of stoneware and fireclay is used by **Ian Sprague** (Australia) to coil-build pots that begin with a shallow bowl form which is thrown to save time. The pots are allowed to stiffen slightly and are then beaten with a paddle to create asymmetrical faces and ridges. Sometimes the surfaces are textured by scraping with combs or saw blades, and pieces of clay are applied and flattened by further beating.

Large hand-built jar form with flared neck, made from laminated stoneware, bone china and porcelain bodies. Height $20\frac{1}{16}$in(56cm). By EWEN HENDERSON (UK), 1980.

Hand-built pot with painted slips, unglazed stoneware. By ELIZABETH FRITSCH (UK).

Hand-built stoneware form with painted slips, unglazed. By ELIZABETH FRITSCH (UK), 1975.

BELOW: Coil-built stoneware pot, matt white glaze with iron oxide and salt solution sprayed over. Height $13\frac{3}{4}$in(35cm). Ash glaze inside. Fired in reduction to 1300°C. By IAN SPRAGUE (Australia), 1980.

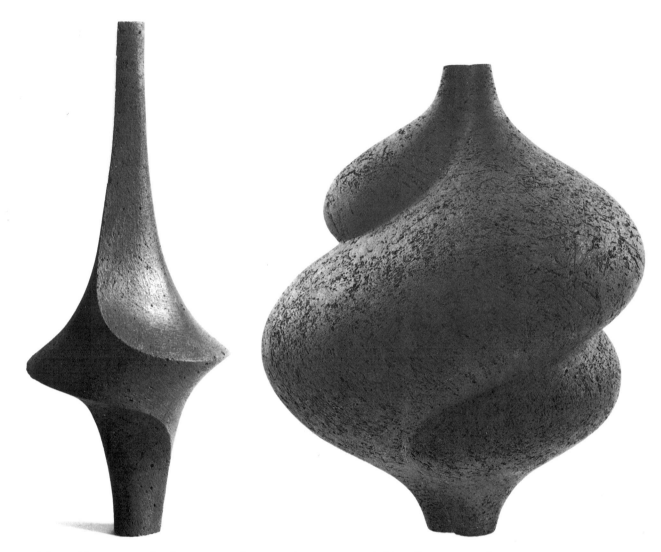

Rick Rudd (New Zealand) may spend several days building one pot by a process of pinching, coiling and scraping. He uses flexible steel scrapers to refine his shapes and to remove pieces of grog from those parts of the surface which he requires to be pitted or textured. He says that his shapes "evolve rather than begin as separate ideas and are *not* taken from nature, although many people see natural forms within them". He prefers one commercially prepared grogged clay from New Zealand to which he adds a coarser grog "for texture rather than strength". A slip, made from white earthenware, and a clear crackle glaze, sometimes with 10% commercial black stain added are the only other materials he uses. These are sufficient (at present) to give contrast between smooth and rough, or between shiny black and white surfaces to complement his unusual vessel forms.

That the "airborne lightness of a bird can be conveyed by defining a volume in a thin, continuous, stressed skin of heavy inert clay never ceases to amaze", says Rosemary Wren (UK), who concentrates upon making hand-built animals and birds in stoneware. She believes that the only vital necessity is for the maker to identify with the bird, so that the feeling comes from within, and that however crude the craftsmanship, if the maker has sufficient intensity of feeling for the living creature then the artefact itself will take on life. "This has nothing to do with copying real life – proportions and surface appearance may be very different – but it has a lot to do with being true to the nature of the material from which it is made." Her partner, Peter Crotty, prepares the clay, paints the colours and fires the kiln. A strong clay body is made by adding fireclay, grog, sand and 'T'material to ECC Hyplas 64 for these animals large and small. Each one is built up from the base by pinching and coiling the clay. Walls are cut and opened out to be filled with another piece of clay, or

Spiral bottle form, hand-built (raku No. 474), fired to 1000°C in a diesel oil fired kiln and smoked in sawdust. Height 19$\frac{11}{16}$in(50cm). By RICK RUDD (New Zealand), 1982.

ABOVE LEFT: Spiral bottle form, hand-built (raku No. 265), fired to 1000°C in a diesel oil fired kiln and smoked in sawdust. Height 9$\frac{7}{16}$in(24cm). Glazed black interior. By RICK RUDD (New Zealand), 1980.

ABOVE: 'Wood Pigeon'. Hand-built stoneware, high clay matt glaze stained with oxides. Length 9in(22.9cm). Fired to 1265°C in an updraught propane gas kiln. By ROSEMARY WREN and PETER CROTTY (UK), 1981.

overlapped and pinched together until the form is resolved. Eventually only a finger-sized hole remains to be filled with a flanged plug of clay smoothed in against the internal air pressure. A slightly flexible 'kidney' rubber is used on both the inside and the outside as the form grows. Profiles are carefully controlled to avoid weak hollows. Finally, holes are made for the eyes "to let the steam out – and the creature looks back".

Wheel-thrown vessels, especially when crisply finished like those by **Nicholas Homoky** (UK) and **Tom Turner** (USA) have a clarity of profile which remains the same viewed from any side. Both these potters work almost exclusively in porcelain which has properties that invite such control and

Porcelain bowl, thrown and turned, with painted rim and design inlaid with stained porcelain slip. Height 6in(15.3cm) approx. Fired to 1260°C in electric kiln, and polished with silicon carbide paper. By NICHOLAS HOMOKY (UK), 1981.

positive treatment. The nature of most stoneware clays appeals to vigorous throwers like **Michael Casson** (UK) whose larger pots exude a sense of the controlled power used to shape them.

Covered jar, porcelain, wheel-thrown, with colour variations from different thicknesses of the apple-ash glaze, fired to cone 9 in reduction. Height 10in(25.4cm). By TOM TURNER (USA), 1981. In the collection of Howard and Edith Jacobs.

Wheel-thrown stoneware jar, with dry ochre glaze. By MICHAEL CASSON (UK).

Robert Winokur (USA) takes traditional utilitarian vessels as his starting-point for further exploration of their sculptural qualities. He tries to do this "without relinquishing the character of their identities". He says that he "still cherishes the thought that it is possible for pottery to reside in museums and hold its own in the company of painting and sculpture, but the more I wrestle with vessels and containers of volumetric proportions, the more I find myself accepting the premise that profound, visually evocative forms must, if they are to succeed in that context, be separated from their association with the history and tradition of utilitarian pottery. The most beautiful of pitchers is always seen in terms of its use first and may never come to be viewed at first sight in terms of its own aesthetic impact".

'Classical Vessel with Stick and Fin' ('Gesture' series). Height 24in(61cm). Salt-glazed stoneware with slips, engobes and blue wood-ash glaze. By ROBERT WINOKUR (USA), 1982.

'Pedestal Piece'. Constructed from thrown stoneware forms (body 50 parts 'T' material; 50 parts porcelain). Height 12in(30.5cm). Reduction fired to 1290°C followed by platinum lustre firing to 750°C. By GLYN HUGO (UK), 1982.

RIGHT: 'Baroque Wall piece No.2', fine-grained red earthenware, moulded, fired to approximately 1040°C and then polished on a lapping wheel with silicon carbide grit. Black terra sigillata slip has been applied to the inner surface and the rim is faced with slate. $13 \times 6\frac{1}{4} \times 7\frac{1}{2}$in ($33 \times 16 \times 19$cm). By MARTIN SMITH (UK), 1981.

Martin Smith (UK) produced some eloquent bowl forms until about 1978 using the raku process with a refinement not usually associated with that technique. Geometric, linear patterns were applied by spraying a white glaze on bisqued ware (made from 'T' material) over masking tape. The glaze was fired to 1000°C and the pieces subjected to reduction in fine sawdust, followed by rapid cooling in water. Thus, the exposed body is blackened, contrasting with the white glaze which is itself heavily crackled with a network of black lines. All too few such pieces had been made when he abandoned raku in favour of working in terracotta clay, again in a unique, inimitable way.

He had long been fascinated by the transformation of clay into stone and felt that, without preconceived attitudes regarding the ethics of the 'truth to materials' approach, there could be no impediment to working upon the shaping of fired clay (given appropriate tools and equipment) any more than when it is still plastic. His exhaustive and perceptive studies of Italian Renaissance art and architecture had developed further directions for him in his committed exploration of form and space. This subsequent fusion of ideas, materials and techniques resulted in a series of vessel forms constructed from press-moulded, redware components, ground and polished on a lapidary wheel with silicon carbide grit. Sections are made from red earthenware, to which grog (made from the same body) has been added, and bonded together with epoxy resin adhesives after firing to 1000°–1050°C. The higher the temperature, the darker the red colour. Tonal patterns on the surface of these pieces are created with a terra sigillata slip of the same clay, stained with oxides, and applied to the bisque before firing again' to a temperature 10°C below that of the first firing. He sometimes incorporates aluminium sheet in these precisely engineered forms, many of which strongly interact with the unusual supporting blocks or plinths that elevate the hollow vessels.

Simple pre-formed clay shapes, either slip-cast or extended, are used extensively by some potters who cut, alter, distort or build with them in a variety of ways. **Kurt Spurey** (Austria) is well known for his work with pre-cast porcelain slabs and box forms which he alters in the plastic state to manipulate the effects of light across surfaces in a fluid way. **Leo King** (New Zealand), on the other hand, cuts into and carves slip-cast spheres to create a shell-like form. He chose to slip-cast in order to obtain consistently thin spheres strong enough to be handled; the carving is done in the white-hard state. The final shape is produced by the deformation or slumping which occurs when the pieces are once-fired (raw-glazed) to 1180°C in an electric kiln. He can control the degree of deformation by the carving, or by varying the thickness of the material.

ABOVE RIGHT: KURT SPUREY (**Austria**) re-shaping a slip-cast porcelain form.

RIGHT: Porcelain vase made from slip-cast slabs, clear glazed by KURT SPUREY (**Austria**).

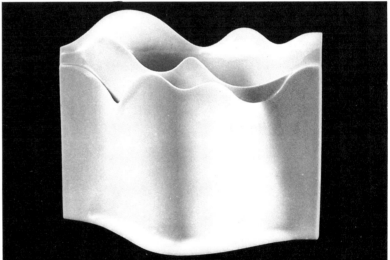

'Lamella Form'. Made from slip-cast white clay sphere with inlaid black lines, glazed black inside, unglazed outside. $9\frac{13}{16} \times 7\frac{1}{16}$in (25 × 18cm). Once fired to 1180°C in an electric kiln which causes the carved sphere to slump in a controlled way producing this form. By LEO KING (New Zealand), 1981.

Oldrich Asenbryl (UK) extrudes porcelain tubes which he bends, curls and assembles into his 'movement sculptures'.

Assembling units into quite complex spatial relationships interests many ceramic sculptors. **Graham Burr** (UK) press-moulded the stoneware tubes for his '12 Arches' sculpture. He admits to having ambivalent feelings towards the medium of ceramics, both liking and disliking what he describes as its·"attractive, sensuous, technical, limited character".

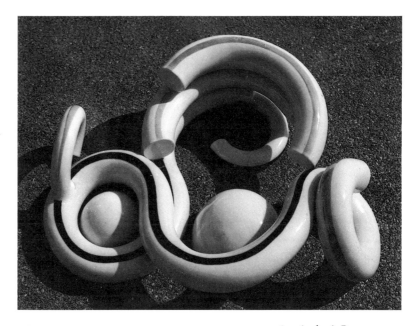

'Constant Movement'. Extruded, press-moulded and assembled porcelain, reduction fired to 1300°C in an oil-fired kiln. 15¾in(40cm). Red and green enamels are then airbrushed on to the fired glaze and the piece re-fired to 840°C. By OLDRICH ASENBRYL (UK), 1981.

'12 Arches'. Press-moulded forms on a slab-built base, with nickel and copper oxides under white glaze (66 parts potash feldspar; 12 parts dolomite; 3 parts bone ash; 18 parts china clay; 5 parts tin oxide); paper-resist and copper glaze. By GRAHAM BURR (UK), 1981.

All the sculptural pieces by **Beate Kuhn** (West Germany) are constructed from separately thrown elements joined together. Such objects would be difficult to realize unless assembled from units in this way. Similarly, the slab sculpture by **Gerald Weigel** (West Germany) appears as an individual object but is made from a number of identically shaped slabs joined around a single axis.

'Climbing Ranks to a Vessel'. Stoneware form constructed from multiple thrown parts. Height $20\frac{1}{16}$in(51cm). Red body with one dark blue glaze, a second slip glaze layer followed by several iron glazes, giving yellow and reddish-brown colours. Fired in electric kiln to cone 6a. By BEATE KUHN (West Germany), 1981.

Slab-built form, grogged stoneware with feldspathic glaze containing iron oxide. Height $9\frac{7}{16}$in(24cm). Reduction fired to 1360°C. By GERALD WEIGEL (West Germany), 1981.

Stoneware pot, with feldspathic glaze containing iron oxide, fired in reduction to 1360°C. Height $7\frac{7}{8}$in(20cm). By GOTLIND WEIGEL (West Germany), 1981.

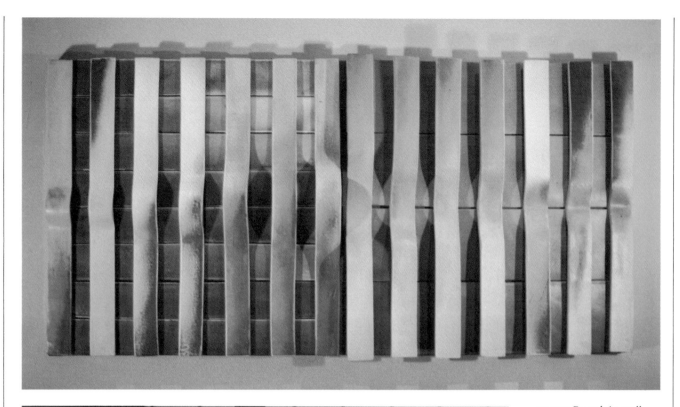

ABOVE: Porcelain wall-piece, hand-built, copper and iron oxides and rutile, sprayed thinly over with barium and feldspathic glazes. 56 × 28in (142.2 × 71.1cm). By RUTH DUCKWORTH (USA), 1981.

Relief sculpture in Schloss Birlinghoven, hand-built stoneware in 32 parts, fired to cone 11 in oxidation with ash and feldspathic glazes. Height 8ft 7½in(2.62m), length 14ft 2⅛in(4.33m). By DIETER CRUMBIEGEL (West Germany), 1978.

Thrown and re-shaped porcelain form with high zinc glaze. Height $12\frac{9}{16}$in(32cm). Colours obtained from cobalt and iron. Reduction fired to 1310°C. By ERIK PLØEN (Norway), 1981.

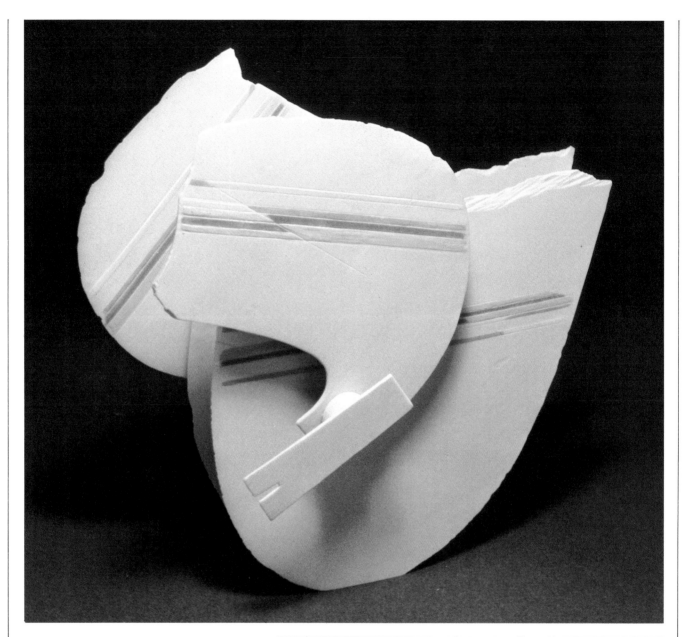

Thin, rolled slabs of porcelain clay, dried and fired extremely slowly to prevent warping are shaped and assembled into delicate relationships by **Eileen Nisbet** (UK). Her 'pot forms' were the simplest pot shape she could imagine – a basic U shape which was a way of describing the form. She wanted to start with a pot shape without making it a 'useful' object. ("Why must I necessarily start with a hole in the middle and build walls all around?") The edges of the slabs are often thinned to make them translucent, sometimes broken edges are contrasted against others that are smooth and flat. The slabs are fired separately and joined to each other when completed by extruded tubular sections of porcelain and strong adhesive.

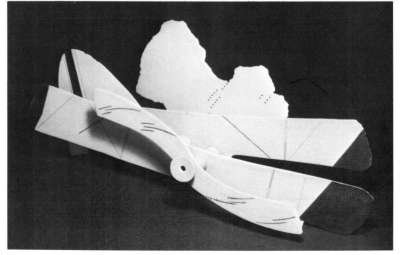

Very large ceramic sculptures can be assembled in a number of ways from individually made and fired sections. **Joan Campbell** (Australia) has produced large forms over 6 ft high which have survived outdoors in college grounds for several years (there is little risk of frost or smog damage in Western Australia). The sections are handbuilt, usually organic forms, with a neck and socket jointing arrangement to allow the parts to fit together neatly with the joint concealed from view within the body of the piece. She prepares a concrete base on site with three reinforcing metal rods cemented in place. Holes drilled through the bottom of the first sculptural section allow it to slip over the rods and about 12 in. of cement is then poured in to fix it securely. Subsequent sections are joined to the first with epoxy resin. Resolving the problem of joining these pieces has, she says, released a flood of ideas for large-scale ceramic sculptures which she intends to explore.

Large earthenware 'totem' forms, made in sections by hand-building methods, green slip-glazed. 6ft 6in(198.1cm) and 5ft 6in(167.7cm). Three similar forms were commissioned for the Presbyterian Ladies College in Perth, 1981. By JOAN CAMPBELL (Australia), 1981.

OPPOSITE ABOVE: 'Pot with Striped Wings'. Porcelain slab construction, inlaid and painted with coloured slips, and assembled after firing to 1240°C in an electric kiln. $9\frac{7}{16} \times 9\frac{1}{16} \times 3\frac{9}{16}$in ($24 \times 23 \times 9$cm). By EILEEN NISBET (UK), 1981.

OPPOSITE BELOW: 'Aeroplane and Cloud'. Porcelain slab construction, inlaid and painted with coloured slips (the cloud is pierced with a drill), and assembled after firing to 1240°C in an electric kiln. $18\frac{1}{8} \times 5\frac{1}{2} \times 5\frac{1}{8}$in($46 \times 14 \times 13$cm). By EILEEN NISBET (UK), 1981.

'Pillar'. Stoneware with sprayed salt solution, fired to cone 6. Height 7ft 6in(228.6cm). By FRANKLYN HEISLER (Canada), 1978.

Franklyn Heisler (Canada) has also produced very large totemic pieces, hand-built, sprayed with salt solutions, and fired to cone 6 in one piece.

The starting-point for the sculptural works of **Michel Kuipers** (Holland) are what he calls "breaking patterns". He challenges the spectator "to read the cracks and broken segments and reconstruct the form". His sculptures are symbolic in that they are analogous to "ancient orders and lost cultures". He describes the work as "an amalgamation of three factors: culture, nature and the element of time. The culture is symbolized by the geometric features of a square, a circle, or a line. These may appear in three-dimensional form as well as in applied colour. They form the linking element in the broken pattern. Nature is suggested in the 'weathering' of the fragments and by the crack itself". Time is expressed by the way in which adjoining pieces vary in tone "as if they each had had a different life after breaking".

ABOVE RIGHT: Fragmented Square'. Stoneware floor-piece, built up solid, then broken and hollowed out when leather-hard.
$32\frac{1}{4} \times 29\frac{1}{2} \times 2\frac{3}{4}$in($82 \times 75 \times 7$cm). Copper slip line. Reduction fired to 1250°C. By MICHEL KUIPERS (Holland), 1979.

'Distorted Pile'. Stoneware, built up hollow by a combination of coiling and pinching. Height $20\frac{7}{8}$in(53cm). Fragments kept separate by paper. With copper slip line. Fired in oxidation to 1250°C. By MICHEL KUIPERS (Holland), 1980.

'Helm'. Slab-built form with matt black manganese engobe, fired in oxidation to 1300°C. Height 20$\frac{1}{16}$in(56cm). By FRITZ VEHRING (West Germany), 1982.

Some of these sculptures are made in solid clay, which is broken up when leather-hard, and then hollowed out. After bisque firing they are separately glazed and individually fired. In some of the standing forms the sections are hollow-built as separate pieces and the 'cracks' are simulated. A layer of toilet paper is inserted between the sections to keep them from sticking together. Either oxidation or reduction atmospheres (or a combination of both) may be used by Michel Kuipers when firing to 1250°C, with glazes based on dolomite-tin-rutile over a copper slip. The human head and figure provide endless material for creative work in ceramics, and the simplest form can be extremely effective, as demonstrated by **Fritz Vehring** (West Germany) with his helmet forms. However, the other extreme of hyper-realism can become a form of abstraction in the hands of a ceramist like **Jan Van Leeuwen** (Holland). He prefers to work by directly casting parts of the male torso in plaster to make one-off moulds into which he presses a French stoneware clay, firing at 1280°C. His main interest is in the movement of bodies, faces and hands and he seeks "to harden something soft and yet preserve its softness". The pieces are occasionally glazed; or the fired surface sand-blasted.

'Fragments'. Mould-made forms, stoneware. Height 11¾in(30cm) approx. The one on the left has been sand-blasted after firing to 1250°C. By JAN VAN LEEUWEN (Holland), 1979.

'Torso'. Mould-made form with barium matt glaze fired to 1250°C. Height 27$\frac{9}{16}$in(70cm). By JAN VAN LEEUWEN (Holland), 1977.

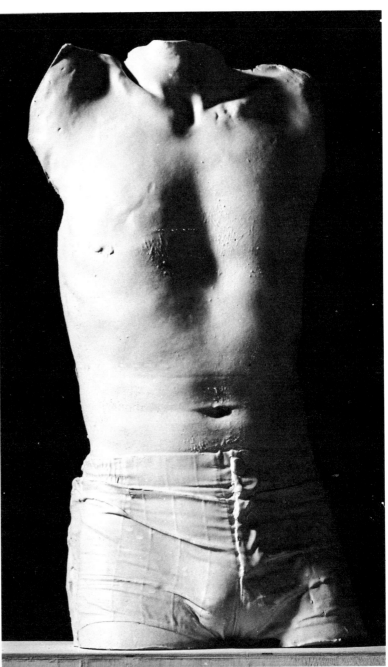

The cool, symbolic images of **Glenys Barton** (UK) are completely modelled by hand before she makes plaster moulds for subsequent slip-casting. Her earlier work, usually in porcelain or bone-china, was similarly slip-cast. It was either glazed with screen-printed colours or left entirely free of glaze and subsequently polished. Such methods allowed her to retain precise control over the final image. This somewhat clinical approach heightens the impression of lonely isolation evoked by many of her pieces in which single male figures are displayed in motionless geometry. More recently Glenys Barton has worked with crackled earthenware glazes that enliven the surfaces of her sculptures with subtle variations of colour and texture. This process, which includes smoking the glazed piece in sawdust, introduces an element of chance into her work but the artist still remains very much in control. **Ann Mortimer** (Canada) used draped slabs of plastic clay to produce her 'Faces of Tranquillity' series, and a

'Lady with Three Faces'. Slip-cast bone china on a marble base. Height 17in(43.2cm). Fired to 1240°C. By GLENYS BARTON (UK), 1981.

'The Faces of Tranquillity' ('Transition' series). Draped slabs; oxides and slips with residual salt firing to cone 3. 9 × 5 × 10in (22.9 × 128 × 25.4cm). By ANN MORTIMER (Canada), 1981.

RIGHT: 'Female head'. Slip-cast, turquoise alkaline glaze (containing copper carbonate), fired to 1040°C. When removed from the electric kiln this glaze has a bright, glossy surface and sand-blasting equipment is used to reduce this to a 'sugary' texture. The piece is then smoked in sawdust to stain and emphasize the crackle. The head, based on the bone structure of the potter Jacqueline Poncelet, is approximately life-size. By GLENYS BARTON (UK) 1982.

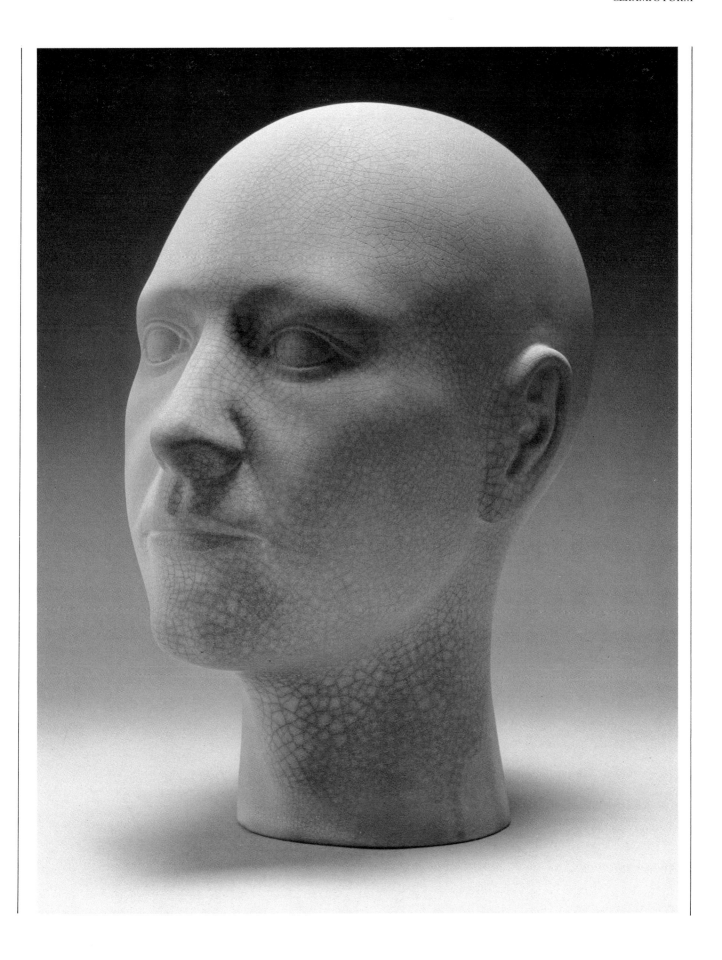

ABOVE: 'Mauve Introvert' (part of a bust).
Hand-built with pieces of plastic clay sheet,
fired in an electric kiln. Height 20$\frac{13}{16}$in(58cm).
By CARMEN DIONYSE (Belgium), 1977.

'Figure'. Slab-built white stoneware form,
unglazed, fired to 1250°C. Height
5ft 11in(1.8m). By MARIA KUCZYNSKA (Poland),
1982.

'Il Vecchio'. Hand-built with pieces of plastic clay sheet, fired in an electric kiln. Height 18⅞in(48cm). By CARMEN DIONYSE (Belgium), 1978.

RIGHT: 'Goalie Icon behind the Goalie's Mask'. Hand-built raku, 23 × 14 × 7½in (58.4 × 35.5 × 19.1cm). By DAVID TORESDAHL (Canada), 1981.

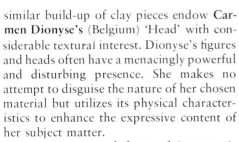

similar build-up of clay pieces endow **Carmen Dionyse's** (Belgium) 'Head' with considerable textural interest. Dionyse's figures and heads often have a menacingly powerful and disturbing presence. She makes no attempt to disguise the nature of her chosen material but utilizes its physical characteristics to enhance the expressive content of her subject matter.

A more animated form of imagery is created by **David Toresdahl** (Canada). He draws constantly and fills many sketchbooks which provide him with starting-points for much of his figurative sculpture. The drawings are not made with three-dimensional work in mind but he uses them "to examine a set of relationships, forms in space, rather than taking an academic approach to drawing". He employs unusual techniques, such as mixing bronze dust with clay to obtain a durable body at cones 2 and 4 which gives colours ranging from tan to black. "This body is impervious to climatic changes and is extremely suitable for outdoor pieces."

A notable proportion of potters who turned away from, or perhaps never even started with, pottery vessels have used clay to explore a fantasy world of strange crea-

'Carved Plate'. Stoneware with pattern incised through black slip to tan body. Fired to cone 8. By DAVID TORESDAHL (Canada), 1982.

BELOW: 'Hills, Trees and Sheep'. Thrown, slabbed and modelled elements in red earthenware clay, matt white glaze coloured with glaze stains dipped, poured and sprayed. Height 14in(35.5cm). Fired in electric kiln to 1100°C. By TESSA FUCHS (UK), 1981.

ABOVE: 'Dragon Dance'. Hand-built stoneware, sprayed with copper, cobalt and manganese oxides, fired to cone 7 with matt white glaze (sprayed). 19 × 15 × 11in(48.3 × 38.1 × 28cm). By NEIL DALRYMPLE (Canada), 1981.

tures, miniature gardens and surreal situations; humorous, whimsical, satirical, even grotesque. The relatively small size of such pieces may cause them to be dismissed as unworthy to figure seriously as ceramic sculpture. Nevertheless, this aspect of ceramics continues to prove popular with the buying public. While there is, undoubtedly, a great deal of inconsequential modelling among much of the work found in craft shops, a few ceramists manage to rise above this mundane level by virtue of their imaginative approach to, and choice of, subject matter, their skill in manipulating materials and processes, and their distinctive style.

'The Dragon's Mistress'. Hand-built stoneware, sprayed with copper, cobalt and manganese oxides, fired to cone 8 bisque followed by matt white glaze sprayed and re-fired to cone 6. Height 18in(45.8cm) approx. By NEIL DALRYMPLE (Canada), 1980.

'Cushion Form'.
Porcelain slip (membrane
formed by soaking
textile fabric), with
modelled additions, fired
to 1280°C in an electric
kiln. By RUTH and ALAN
BARRATT-DANES (UK),
1981.

'Cushion Form' (detail).
Porcelain. By RUTH and
ALAN BARRATT-DANES
(UK), 1981.

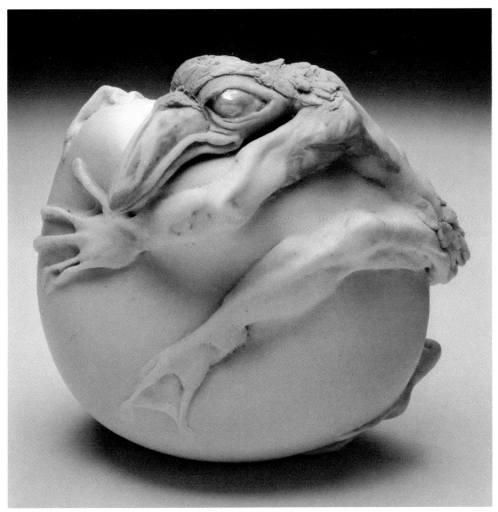

'Predator Pot'. Thrown and modelled porcelain with inlaid coloured clay fired to 1260°C in an electric kiln. Height 4in(10.2cm) approx. By RUTH and ALAN BARRATT-DANES (UK), 1982.

Ruth and Alan Barratt-Danes (UK) work together on ideas which arise from complex, interwoven experiences and thoughts formulated over many years. They acknowledge influences such as Bosch, Dürer, Brueghel, Blake and others from both graphic and literary sources, but with the underlying theme concerning the metaphorical relationship of two components: figure and object. "The work uses this metaphorical element to present strange and alienating ideas that are meant not to charm but to surprise and, sometimes, to shock and, therefore, to produce its full effect, the object must at least keep a foothold in a territory that the observer is familiar with. By the anthropomorphizing of various animals it is possible to combine human and animal characteristics, and the strangely threatening personalities that evolve are used to express some of our less desirable human foibles."

A recent series of 'predator' pots is typical of their work. The underlying form supporting the frog-like creature is initially thrown as a totally enclosed porcelain pot which is allowed to stiffen. This is then softened with a damp sponge just enough for the modelling to be completed, so that the creature appears to be impressing "his physical will on the structure". The air trapped inside the enclosed form acts as a cushion, but it is at this stage that many pieces are lost "because it is essential to retain a tensile elasticity in the structure supporting the creature". Finally, the form is cut into two parts with an undulating line, and a flange is coiled and shaped inside. Plastic porcelain body is stained and used to colour parts of the creature. Following a soft bisque to 1000°C the second firing is taken to 1240°C.

Another interesting technique used by the Barratt-Danes and others enables them to produce their 'cushion forms'. Since they work mainly in a representational way, they exploit techniques which will create the mood and feeling of a situation. By making a particular form, such as an armchair, in soft textile material, filling this with cushion filler (plastic foam chippings) and thoroughly soaking the whole piece in slip for a few minutes (repeated two or three times to build up sufficient thicknesses of clay) they have the basic support for subsequent modelling. The cushion is allowed to dry a little before it is manipulated into the final form. It is then secured in position While further additions are made and the whole is left to dry in the normal way. The work is fired to 1280°C and the 'fabric' membrane is then strong enough to handle. (It is important to ensure efficient ventilation of the kiln room during firing as the fumes given off by the burning fabric and foam are toxic.)

Tony Bennett (UK) considered taking up a career in illustration but got side-tracked into clay. He was particularly interested in the work of cartoonists such as Gerald Scarfe and Ralph Steadman, "who played around with the human figure, distorting various elements into completely new forms, whilst retaining the recognizable essence of the original person". Later, he discovered American underground comics which he found brash, bawdy and full of energy, life and superb draughtsmanship. American

ABOVE RIGHT: 'Green Boots'. Slip-cast earthenware, glazed, with underglaze colours. Height 9in(22.9cm). By TONY BENNETT (UK).

'Teapot'. White earthenware clay stained with blue glaze stain, pressed into the mould, the mould filled with red earthenware slip and cast. Fired to 1160°C. Height 5in(12.7cm). By TONY BENNETT (UK).

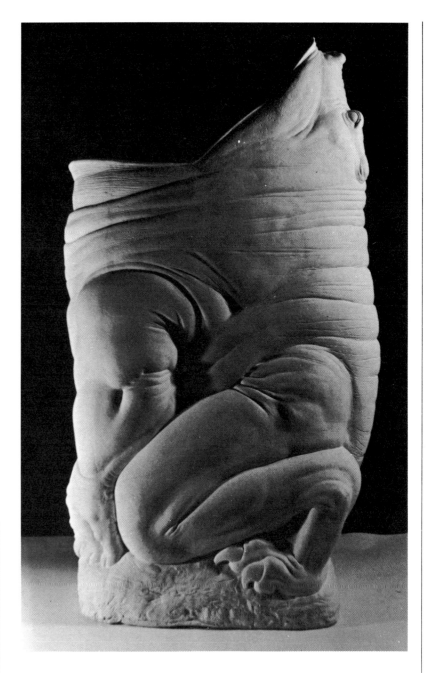

'Seduction of the Innocent'. Unglazed porcelain, slip-cast, hand-built and slip-impregnated fabric, fired to 1300°C. Height 23⅝in(60cm). By ALAN WATT (Australia).

Funk ceramics were becoming known in Britain about this time and, through attending a series of lectures as a student, he felt tremendously excited as he had seen nothing like them before and had never even considered making such pieces. These and other experiences led to a period of detailed modelling – a gorilla (after a week spent drawing in Dudley Zoo), pigs, "Hell's Angels, skinheads and cops because they were around at the time"; but later he began to explore things more akin to fantasy. These were composite figures, anthropomorphics, essences of things which interested him. "Evolution excites me – the idea that

'Gulper'. Press-moulded using 'T' material, fired to 1160°C. Height 24in(61cm). This piece was commissioned by the South East Regional Arts Association for a touring exhibition. By TONY BENNETT (UK).

one form mutates into another to accommodate new conditions. One can imagine a simple, single-cell creature swimming around in a primordial soup, and one can have a fair idea of most of the other life forms sharing the earth with us now but, considering the immense time span involved, and the endless changes and bizarre forms there must have been, there is a very rich vein of imagery.''

His main working methods are coil-building, press-moulding and slip-casting. He finds that coil-building a figure is a very intense exercise. "It requires sustained concentration and a strong impression" of what he wants to achieve. Without such an impression he prefers to work on a solid clay model from which a plaster mould is made for subsequent slip-casting or pressing. The moulds are used not to mass-produce pieces, but so that he can make a few variations or create certain decorative effects which are only possible by the use of moulds. All his work is earthenware (bisque 1160°C and glost 1060°C) because an important aspect is colour, and earthenware offers the widest possible spectrum.

To **Delan Cookson** (UK), the absurd and the fantastic appear to be just beneath the surface of the real world, and the most fruitful source of material for his sculptural pieces are everyday objects, such as tools, that serve some basic function (such as tightening or squeezing) and that, when taken out of context, are capable of completely new meaning. He says that: "Whilst I respond and admire the monumentality, the stillness, and sensitivity to surface qualities achieved by Brancusi, I am also attracted by the disturbing elements of Magritte." For him, clay seems an ideal material for interpreting qualities of softness, yet it is equally able to depict hard-edged, rigid and stable forms. The combination of these visual elements continues to provide him with material for formulating basic ideas.

Each of his 'entertainment' pieces presents him with fresh technical problems. In many of his ceramic sculptures he includes glass. For his 'Jelly Press' (p. 132), the glass jelly was blown into a mould, but for 'Portnoy's Complaint No. 1' (p. 9), the ceramic parts were thrown, distorted, fired, glazed and assembled first so that accurate measurements could be taken before the casual-looking dribbles of glass could be made. The hot glass is formed over a metal pattern and many attempts are usually necessary to achieve the desired result. Only

'Jelly Press'. Slab-built stoneware with thrown additions and blown-glass 'jelly' (blown into a mould). By DELAN COOKSON (UK), 1981.

after the glass has been annealed and cooled is it fitted to the ceramic. The subject matter was a recognizable screw press, water pumps and a squashed toothpaste tube.

Within certain technical constraints, contemporary ceramics impose very few restrictions on those who choose to work in clay. Although the 'art' of ceramics in the West has not yet been accorded the unstinting respect and status that it has enjoyed for

Lidded porcelain jar, wheel-thrown, dipped in cornish stone glaze, underglaze bands of cobalt applied, over which further glaze is sprayed to achieve the necessary thickness to produce widely spaced crackle lines. Height $3\frac{1}{16}$in(8cm). Fired to Orton cone 11 in reduction atmosphere. Lines stained with 22 carat gold (to produce the pink colour) and brush-banded gold. By GARY WORNELL (UK), 1980.

Wheel-thrown porcelain form with high zinc/barium glaze containing rutile, and crystalline matt surface. Height $8\frac{1}{4}$in(21cm). Colour obtained from nickel oxide. Fired in oxidation to 1280°C. By INGVIL HAVREVOLD (Norway), 1981.

centuries in the East, there is a refreshing freedom now (which some may find disturbing), and a growing confidence among artist-potters who wish to resolve ideas and feelings, expressing themselves through clay, regardless of any pressure to make objects that will sell. **Jan de Rooden** (Holland) is one of those who felt compelled to abandon allegiance to traditional attitudes towards ceramics. Prior to 1980 his approach to his work was dominated by attempting to "live up to the classic ceramic qualities from the East and from the West" which he "admired and enjoyed". This required him to adapt his work consciously towards those ideals already long in existence. Becoming aware of an increasing urge to find a completely fresh and personal approach, to discover a more independent self in ceramics ("that could come to life, because I live"), he knew that for him "those ceramics should have a clear palette and a clean shape, there ought to be colour and the idiom of the total should relate" to his own social and geographical environment. Developing these new directions continues to be "a very slow progress along a somewhat lonesome road". Although his current pieces take longer to complete, so that

communication through the finished work has been reduced since 1980, he is compensated by a feeling of greater satisfaction and improvement in the "quality of life".

Spheres, cubes, pyramids and rectilinear forms often feature in Jan de Rooden's meticulously constructed ceramic sculptures but they rarely appear as static objects. Movement or change (sometimes violent) seems to be affecting their very existence. These forms, often suggesting tension or stress, may be slab-built or combined with wheel-thrown elements in stoneware clay.

'Cycle II' (accents in red and black). Slab-built oxidised stoneware fired to 1260°C. Height $14\frac{3}{16}$in(36cm), width $26\frac{3}{8}$in(67cm). By JAN DE ROODEN (Holland), 1982.

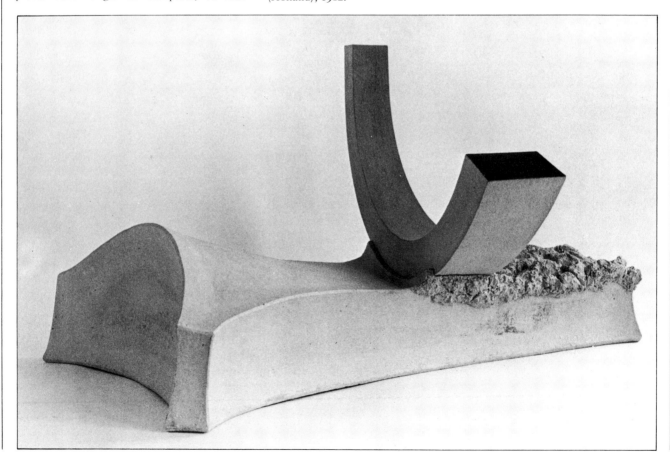

'Shadow of Civilisation IV'. Slab-built oxidised stoneware fired to 1260°C.
Width 13in(33cm). By JAN DE ROODEN (Holland), 1981.

BELOW: 'Project for an Environment'. Slip-cast terracotta. $41\frac{5}{16} \times 16\frac{1}{2} \times 8\frac{5}{8}$in.
($105 \times 42 \times 22$cm). Reduction fired to cone 06. By NINO CARUSO (Italy), 1979.

A rather more light-hearted approach to clay is taken by **Alan Heaps** (UK). Having been trained as a graphic artist, and without any formal training in ceramics, he does not feel bound by past traditions. Feeling free to work as he pleases, he has evolved his own working methods using tools such as set squares, compasses, dowel rods, twist drills and wood augers, in addition to the more usual equipment of a pottery workshop. His work is a distillation of many interests including animals and plants (he grows hundreds of cacti and succulents), ancient cultures, architecture and primitive engineering. The last of these is evident in many of his highly individual pieces. He makes many drawings around a particular idea, the drawings themselves suggesting new directions. Working with clay is a continuation of this process, involving much construction, destruction and rearrangements. Endless possibilities present themselves, so that he may eventually reach a stage where ideas for another piece become strong. This suggests starting afresh, which he finds both frustrating and exciting.

RIGHT: 'Hanging Garden'. White stoneware, orange-yellow slip decoration, glazed with turquoise-green barium matt glaze poured over a yellow high clay matt glaze. Width 14in(35.6cm). Fired in oxidation to 1280°C. By ALAN HEAPS (UK), 1981.

'Cannon'. Stoneware, slip decoration and matt glazes fired to 1260°C. Length 12in(30.5cm). The smoke is made from a chocolate-black body as are the cannonballs which are rubbed with iron spangles. The metal rod holding the cannonball is painted as a dotted line, cartoon-style. The cannon moves along and the barrel will move upon the carriage. By ALAN HEAPS (UK), 1981.

Diane Peach (Australia) uses various forms of construction for her decorative ceramic sculptures. The slab-roller plays a large part in influencing what she makes because she finds that rolling a slab of clay is effortless, with almost any size being possible. (She often makes a slab and wonders what to do with it!) Working mainly in porcelain, she uses deflocculated casting slip for joining clay parts together because the water content is much less than in slurry, so that shrinkage is reduced, placing less strain on the joints. Since it is also of a slimy, gluey consistency, pieces stick firmly on contact, with little else besides the touch of a damp sponge. Slip can be thickened by adding vinegar if a thicker paste is needed. She also makes slabs by quickly pouring casting slip on to a smooth plaster board. "These are thin and flexible, due to the thixotropic qualities of casting slip, and easy to drape into irregular moulds, for with agitation of the clay it will sag into deep contours."

'Noah at Sea'. Stoneware, coiled and slabbed construction with modelled animals. $25\frac{9}{16} \times 13\frac{3}{4} \times 8\frac{11}{16}$in($65 \times 35 \times 22$cm). Glaze contains equal parts china clay, feldspar and barium carbonate, to which 10–14% copper oxide is added (some spots unglazed). The waves are dipped in dilute glaze by holding one corner to give gradation of colour from white to dark green. Fired in oil kiln with minimal reduction to Orton cone 9. The various elements are then fixed to a stained, polished timber board with epoxy resin adhesive. By DIANE PEACH (Australia), 1981.

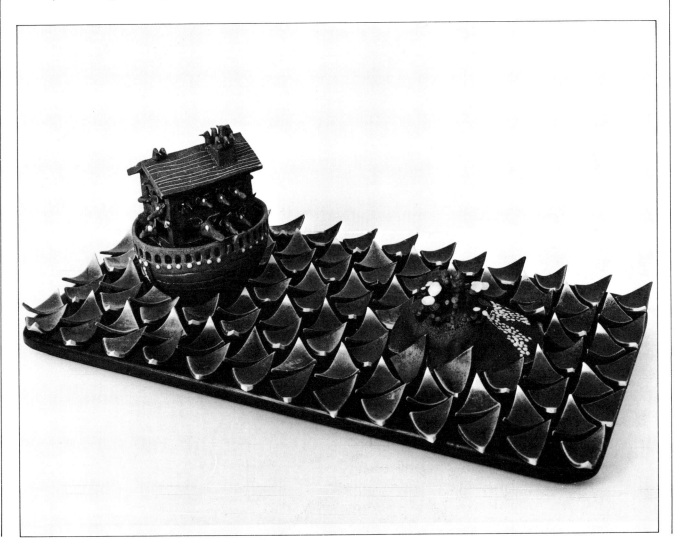

4 DECORATION

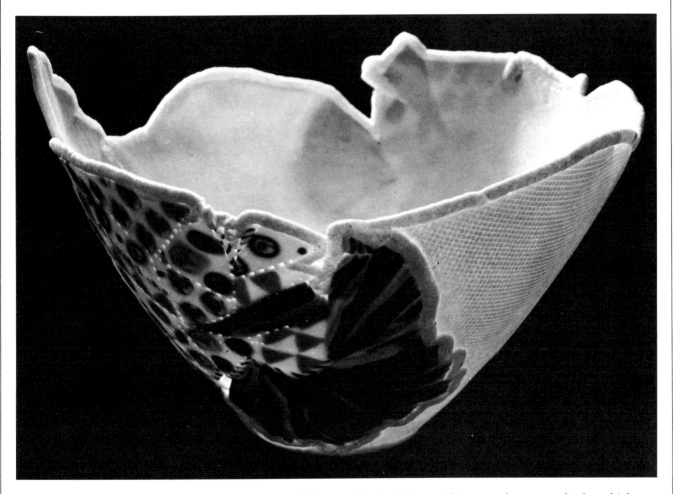

Clay worked in the soft, plastic state can retain evidence of the slightest pressure. Fingerprints of potters working centuries ago have been hardened and fixed in their fired wares for us still to see today. The finer textured bodies lend themselves to extremely detailed work in the hands of a skilled craftsman. Porcelains especially will reveal even minute surface scratches under a coloured transparent glaze such as a celadon.

Hand-built porcelain bowl form, with impressed texture and coloured inlays. Diameter 7in (17..m) approx. The basic body is 40 parts feldspar; 30 parts china clay; 10 parts nepheline syenite; and 10 parts flint. Fired to 1270°C precisely, at which temperature the body begins to melt so that the bowl must be supported in cast saggar. By CURTIS AND SUSAN BENZLE (USA), 1982.

OPPOSITE: Tulip-shaped vessel, porcelain, slab-built and modelled. Height 10¼in (26cm). Outer surface has engraved lines ochre-stained and semi-matt glaze. Inside has manganese pink matt glaze. Fired to 1300°C in oxidation. By JOHANNES GEBHARDT (West Germany), 1982.

Coarser bodies, to which granules of fired clay (grog) or sand are added, invite a more robust treatment and have an appeal of their own, which attracts many ceramists who prefer not to hide natural surface qualities beneath a glaze. Such bodies are less likely to warp or slump in the kiln and they are particularly appropriate for large-scale work and architectural murals. Some of the most exciting applications of such material can be seen in the work of **Ulla Viotti** (Sweden), who combines striking textural qualities in the rhythmic manipulation of plastic clay sheets for large wall panel compositions. Crevices appear in the surface as the clay is bent and stretched. This texture is further emphasized with cobalt or iron oxides (sometimes in combination) which

RIGHT: 'The Wall'. Stoneware mural of relief figures, with iron and cobalt oxides in texture, unglazed. 2ft 9½in × 2ft $\frac{9}{16}$in (85 × 65cm). Fired to 1280°C in an electric kiln. By ULLA VIOTTI (Sweden), 1978.

'Helm'. Slab-built stoneware, scraped surface inlaid with iron oxide. Height 13⅜in (34cm). Fired in oxidation to 1300°C. By FRITZ VEHRING (West Germany), 1980.

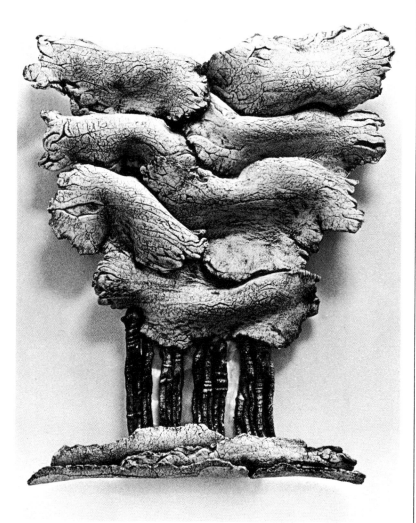

'Between Sky and Earth' (with human figures between). Slabbed and manipulated stoneware with the texture picked out with cobalt oxide. Fired in an electric kiln to 1280°C. By ULLA VIOTTI (Sweden).

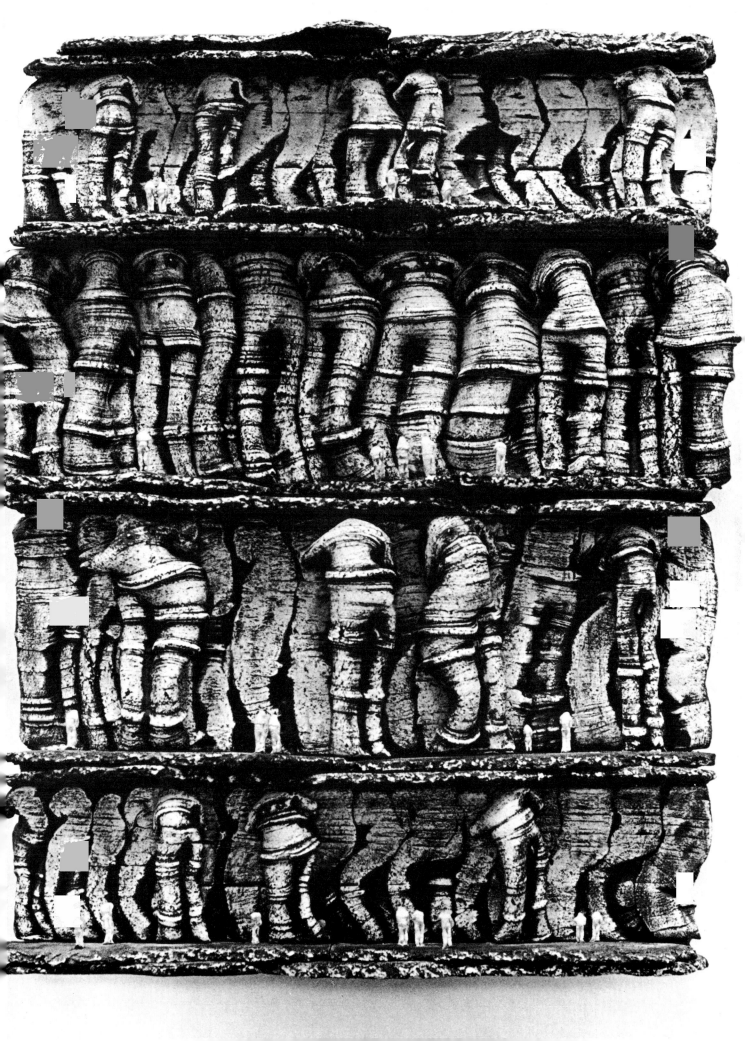

are brushed on the dry, unfired clay. Steel wool is used to remove excess oxide, leaving the cracks stained with dark colour.

Other textures of a more organized appearance can be made by beating plastic clay slabs with wooden battens or paddles before bending and coaxing the slabs into new forms. Another method involves placing pieces of plastic clay, possibly in the form of coils, strips or cut shapes, on top of a rolled-out slab and pressing them together flat with a roller. The edges of the inlaid pieces (if not rolled in too much) retain a fine contour line which can then be stained with oxides as previously described.

Another technique evolved by **Len Castle** (New Zealand) for his organic forms, and one which he has continued to use since 1958, requires the use of very plastic lumps and sheets of clay coated with dry, powdered clay. Thus prepared, the material is then rolled, beaten, cut, stretched, compressed and manipulated. The soft inner clay reacts with the more rigid, dry clay at the surface, and rich textures and patterns are developed. Although he has no conscious desire to emulate the forms of nature, years of living in close association with sea, bush and landscape continue to guide Len Castle's work towards the creation of objects which evoke aspects of certain natural forms and surfaces.

LEFT: Stoneware vase, made from press-moulded slabs, incised and decorated with slips and oxides. Height $27\frac{9}{16}$in (70cm). Fired in an electric kiln to 1240°C. By ANTOINE DE VINCK (Belgium).

BELOW LEFT: 'Landscape'. Hand-built stoneware with inlaid oxides and slips giving black, brick-red, turquoise-green and sand colours to the piece. Height $19\frac{1}{2}$in (49.5cm). Fired to 1270°C in an electric kiln. By JOHNNY ROLF (Holland), 1980.

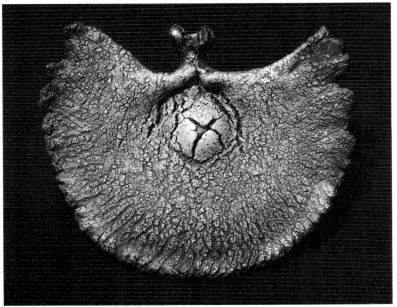

Hanging piece, white stoneware, rolled and hand-stretched construction out of a solid lump of clay, later hollowed. Height 11in (28cm). Exterior unglazed but bisqued form washed with burnt umber pigment. Firing, oxidation/reduction in oil-fired kiln to 1300°C. By LEN CASTLE (New Zealand), 1982.

The ceramic sculptures of **Antoine Richard Crül** (Belgium) are positive, with firm profiles, but considerable visual and tactile interest is contributed by textural and patterned areas. Working in stoneware clays in an almost painterly fashion, he is quick to use any "accidental textures" that occur while work is in progress if he feels that they will add to the expressive power of the form.

This is a happy marriage between intuition and intellectual control. In 'Woman with Cape' (below) he has also used incised linear patterns, drawn in the damp clay, to define areas which he has later stained with oxides. Parts of the cape also retain the clear impression of the cloth or hardboard backing upon which slabs have been rolled out.

'Woman with Cape'. Slab-built stoneware, impressed, incised and inlaid with oxides. Height 2ft 5$\frac{15}{16}$in (76cm). Reduction fired in gas kiln to 1280°C. By ANTOINE RICHARD CRÜL (Belgium), 1977.

Hand-built pot, raku
No. 460, burnished after
scraping, clear glaze
with 10% black stain on
inside and on wavy line.
$11\frac{13}{16} \times 13\frac{3}{4}$in (30 × 35cm).
By RICK RUDD (New
Zealand), 1982.

Contrasting rough, smooth and shiny areas have been outlined in a similar manner by **Rick Rudd** (New Zealand) on his spherical raku pot. Coarse grog liberally added to the clay is torn from the surface as the coiled form is scraped and refined. Smooth areas are burnished or painted with slip or glaze.

Mary White (UK), now living and working in West Germany, is well-known for her fine wheel-thrown work (especially bowls) in porcelain which is often decorated with calligraphy. Recently, she has pursued new directions through hand-building methods, partly as a reaction against the potter's wheel, and partly because she wished to explore further the finer qualities of porcelain. Her 'wrapped' forms resulted from experiments with paper-thin sheets of porcelain and stoneware clays built up in layers ("like torn paper") in a search for luminous effects. The almost random edges of these overlapping sheets are stained with oxides for greater emphasis. This work has no deep psychological meaning but was produced "in the natural process of learning". When glazing these pieces she visualized "fine layers of earth with mysterious metals staining the edges and cracks, and minute specks of gold glistening in the depths". Gold

Hand-built porcelain bowl, tinted brown on white, traces of gold lustre.
Diameter 6in (15.2cm). By MARY WHITE (UK), 1982.

OPPOSITE: 'Queen'. Slab-built stoneware, with slip and oxides, unglazed.
Height $25\frac{9}{16}$in (65cm). Reduction fired to 1280°C. By ANTOINE RICHARD CRÜL
(Belgium), 1978.

lustre, sparingly painted in touches, "to catch the light and suggest riches hidden in earth", increases the illusion. "The use of gold is symbolic, or as a highlight, certainly not meant to be thought of as a form of decoration."

Slabs of porcelain rolled out into thin sheets into which have been pressed some slip trailings (partially dried to a plastic condition on a plaster bat) are wrapped around and joined to create the tall tube pots of **Alan Watt** (Australia). The thin, peripheral, recessed lines have been washed over with cobalt oxide, and the surface wiped clean to reveal the textural interest. The large strip-built covered jar (*right*) by **Henry Lyman** (USA) has also received clay additions to suggest vegetation and clouds. ("This piece was formed as ash from the Mount St Helen's eruption was falling in our yard.") But in this case the piece was bisqued and glazed. Removing glaze from the raised portions brings them into sharp relief.

FAR LEFT: 'Porcelain Tubes'. Slab-built, with rolled-in slip trailings outlined with cobalt wash, clear-glazed interior, unglazed exterior, fired to 1300°C in light reduction (gas kiln). Height of tallest 17in (43.2cm). By ALAN WATT (Australia), 1981.

LEFT: Covered jar, porcelain, hand-built, barium glaze, fired to cone 10. Height 30in (76.2cm). By HENRY LYMAN (USA), 1980.

Porcelain form thrown with rolled rim left unglazed. Height 4½in (12cm). Bright, feldspathic glaze with copper oxide. Reduction fired to 1360°C. By URSULA SCHEID (West Germany), 1981.

Wall bottle, stoneware, textured surface ochre-washed and part-brushed with manganese dioxide, fired to cone 10 in a diesel oil kiln. Diameter 15¾in (40cm). By PETER STICHBURY (New Zealand), 1972. In the collection of Mr & Mrs B. Trussell.

Peter Stichbury (New Zealand) is a production potter who also enjoys making large 'wall pots' with applied textural patterns in clay on forms built from thrown and joined sections. Small pellets of plastic clay deliberately placed and smoothed on to the form, then further pressed into position with a circular stamp, create a very positive pattern (*above*). Other textures are introduced on large platters with a "marvellously impure iron sand from one of West Auckland's West Coast beaches". The sand pattern is freely and quickly applied on to glaze while still wet from pouring or dipping the piece. Stamped, impressed, incised, cut

'Opera Box'. Stoneware and porcelain, with on-glaze enamels and gold lustre. Height 11in (28cm). By HILARY BROCK (UK), 1980.

'General'. Stoneware, thrown and modelled elements. Height 8in (20.3cm). By HILARY BROCK (UK), 1980.

and modelled plastic clay is used in the humorous figurative pieces by **Hilary Brock** (UK). He sometimes employs porcelain and stoneware clays together to provide a greater contrast. The white porcelain offers an ideal ground for painting and he uses water-bound on-glaze enamel colours in a variety of thicknesses. Children's stick-printing stencilling outfits and old ball-point pens are some of his favourite tools. Clay is also patterned by rolling out over material such as plastic doilies. 'Hair' is produced by pushing soft clay through the mesh of a metal tea-strainer. Stoneware clay is more likely to be used for those parts of a piece

'Love Seat'. White porcelain and porcelain stained with copper oxide. 9 × 9in (22.9 × 22.9cm) approx. The potter's description: "The couple, nude and enveloped with strands of porcelain. Like time and webbing, holding them." By GILLIAN STILL (UK), 1981.

'Tower Block'. Stoneware, slab-built construction with thrown and cut additions. 13 × 11in (33 × 28cm). Dry wood-ash glaze (50 parts ash; 50 parts china clay). By BRYAN NEWMAN (UK).

BELOW: 'Boat'. Stoneware, slab-built with superstructure of cut and pierced pieces. Length 9in (22.9cm). Glaze: 20 parts feldspar; 40 parts whiting; 80 parts china clay; 5 parts borocalcite; 4 parts yellow ochre. By BRYAN NEWMAN (UK).

which support or frame the porcelain figures. **Bryan Newman** (UK) spends most of his time making thrown domestic ware and he describes this activity as "a relaxing way of making a living". Occasionally, however, he is able to turn his mind to his distinctive sculptural work. He hopes to keep the imagery fairly fresh by thus apportioning his time, while ensuring that the work remains an enjoyable experience. Although many of these latter pieces may be identified as bridges, boats or buildings, he is mainly interested in dealing with abstract qualities and organizing shapes and textures. This usually involves constructing the object with a slab-built base to which are added many thrown and cut pieces of clay at the leather-hard stage. Wood-ash glazes, very 'dry' in appearance and touch, complement these forms.

There have been an overwhelming number of frilly, fungoid-looking objects produced over the last decade or so, especially since porcelain became popular among studio potters. There is, undoubtedly, a certain sensual pleasure to be obtained by the pinching, wetting and pulling of a smooth clay until it is formed into wafer-thin sheets with random edges. It can then be ruffled as it stiffens, rather like cloth, as **Sylvia Hyman** (USA) has done with stoneware and porcelain elements in her 'Sporophyll' series (*above*). Smaller, individually made fragments of porcelain of

Stoneware and porcelain form on marble base, 'Sporophyll' series. Height 14in (35.5cm). by SYLVIA HYMAN (USA), 1981.

similar appearance have been added to coarse stoneware objects by many potters for textural variation. **Erik Pløen** (Norway) has made vertical forms surmounted by an organized arrangement of strongly textured clay sheets, while **Ruth Duckworth** (USA) used applied additions in quite a different way for her impressive stoneware mural (240 sq. ft) for the Dresdner Bank in Chicago.

ABOVE: Hand-built porcelain form with iron-brown decoration and wax-resist under transparent glaze. Height 7½in (19cm). Reduction fired to 1300°C. By ERIK PLØEN (Norway), 1981.

BELOW: Hand-built porcelain form with green and brown zinc glaze, fired in reduction to 1300°C. Height 11¹³⁄₁₆in (30cm). By ERIK PLOEN (Norway).

'Wall-piece'. Stoneware with copper oxide wash and three glazes. Width 42in (106.7cm). By RUTH DUCKWORTH (USA), 1979.

BELOW: 'Clouds over Lake Michigan'. Stoneware mural, slab construction with colour washes of copper, iron and nickel oxides and four glazes. 24 × 10ft (7.2 × 3.05m) approx. By RUTH DUCKWORTH (USA), 1976. Situated in Dresdner Bank, Chicago.

Flattened coils are applied to slab clay in a strong flowing design in **Antoine de Vinck's** (Belgium) wall panel 'Soul Mirror', while he uses twisted and flattened coils in different coloured clays for his large dish (*below*).

'Soul Mirror'. Hand-built and assembled on an iron plate, stoneware with oxides, matt glaze and gold lustre. $19\frac{11}{16} \times 19\frac{11}{16}$in ($50 \times 50$cm). Wood fired. By ANTOINE DE VINCK (Belgium).

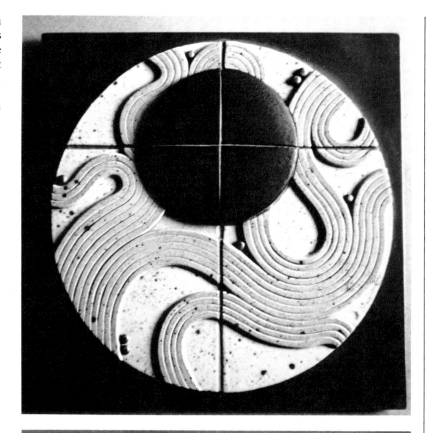

Large stoneware dish with two-coloured twisted clay coils pressed on base and the whole finished on the wheel. Diameter $17\frac{7}{16}$in (45cm). Transparent glaze fired to $1240°$C in an electric kiln. By ANTOINE DE VINCK (Belgium).

BELOW: 'Flounder' hand-built in stoneware clay with porcelain in surface texture. Fired to Orton cone 9. Length $19\frac{3}{4}$in (50cm). By JACK LAIRD (New Zealand) 1981.

'Ceramic Column'. Stoneware, hand-built in six sections with a whitish salt glaze, fixed on to a steel core. Height 7ft 10½in (240cm). By ROY COWAN (New Zealand), 1982. This piece was designed for the Reserve Bank of New Zealand building in Auckland.

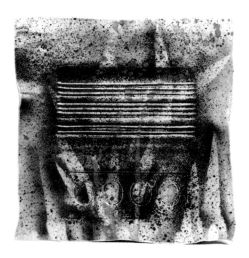

Porcelain plate, stamped slab with feldspathic glaze fired to cones 9–10 in oxidation. 12 × 12in (30.5 × 30.5cm). By MAURICE SAVOIE (Canada), 1977.

Mural in red stoneware, built from slabs and extrusions. 20 × 9ft (6 × 2.74m). Reduction fired to 1260°C. By MAURICE SAVOIE (Canada), 1978/9.

Extruded pieces of clay pressed into, or luted on to, slabs cut into square tiles form the basis of the strong relief pattern in the stoneware mural in Quebec by **Maurice Savoie** (Canada), but a single sheet of plastic porcelain is used for his plate (*left*) into which the linear design has been firmly stamped. Indented surfaces and stamped impressions, delicately colour-washed with oxides and body stains to pick out the surface patterning on the white porcelain sculptures by **Peter Simpson** (UK), render subtle qualities which are further enhanced by the use of wax polishing rather than glazing. The colour is applied after bisque firing to 1000°C. Finally fired to 1240°C–1250°C in an electric kiln, such pieces are then carefully rubbed down with a fine grade of 'wet and dry' carborundum paper. This gives an extremely smooth polish whether wax is used or not. (A good range of similar silicon-carbide-faced papers of various grades are obtainable under different trade names.)

RIGHT: 'First Messenger' Hand-built porcelain with body stains and underglaze pigments, unglazed but polished. Height 15in (38.1cm) approx. Fired in oxidation to 1240°C. By PETER SIMPSON (UK), 1981.

Traditional techniques for treating clay surfaces, such as scratching through a coating of coloured slip to reveal the underlying body, or cutting into and removing some of the surface layer possibly to permit the inlay of a different colour clay, are widely used by potters in many parts of the world. This is a very direct working method allowing close contact and control, so that extremely precise drawing can be sharply detailed. **West Marshall** (UK) enjoys treating some of his pieces with decorative motifs cut and stamped in the leather-hard clay using a knife, boxwood tools and wooden stamps. (Potters also use stamps of plaster or fired clay – both of which are easily made.) Dark-coloured brown slip was brushed and blobbed into his dish (*right*) and the surplus carefully scraped away when almost dry. Scraping away can cause smudging of the design if undertaken too soon, but if left

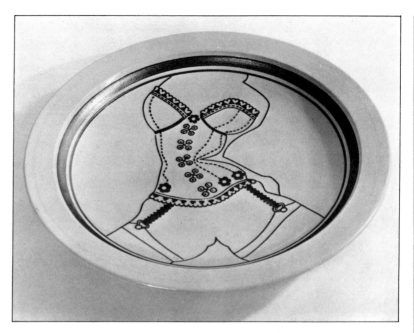

Porcelain dish, thrown, cut and stamped decoration inlaid with brown slip under translucent white glaze. Diameter $9\frac{7}{16}$in (24cm). Reduction fired to 1260°C. The basic white slip to which colouring oxides are added consists of 50 parts china clay (for whiteness); 20 parts SMD ball clay (to give adhesion); and 30 parts quartz (for whiteness and to decrease shrinkage). By WEST MARSHALL (UK), 1980.

Mug and bowl, thrown and turned, painted and inlaid with black slip on white porcelain. $11 \times 6\frac{11}{16}$in (28×17cm) and $4\frac{5}{16} \times 5\frac{1}{2}$in ($11 \times 14$cm). By NICHOLAS HOMOKY (UK), 1980.

until completely dry the slip tends to become dislodged from the grooves. For this particular colour he finds that a reduction firing is essential to bring the iron content of the slip to the surface. Under oxidizing conditions the decoration would have been only faintly visible. The decorative band, in the form of a female torso, is cut boldly across the centre of the dish and filled as a detailed arrangement of lines and shapes to contrast with the plain 'background'.

Similar clarity of line is achieved by **Nicholas Homoky** (UK) in using an inlaid black slip on white porcelain. After bisque firing between 900°C and 1000°C, he rubs down the inlay to remove scum from the slip before re-firing to the maturing temperature of 1260°C. These pots are carefully turned after throwing so that he can exploit a surface clear from any irregularities which might interfere with the drawing.

ABOVE: 'The Outback Dreamer'. Slabbed earthenware, incised and painted with underglaze stains and low-fire glazes. $26\frac{3}{8} \times 29\frac{9}{16}$in ($67 \times 65$cm). By VINCENT MCGRATH (Australia), 1981.

'Kilburn Pot'. Porcelain, thrown and cut when leather-hard. Height 5in (12.7cm). Ceramic pencil and underglaze colours, clear matt glaze thinly sprayed. Fired to 1260°C in oxidation. By RUTH FRANKLIN (UK).

'Zazie'. Slab-built
stoneware, iron and ash
glaze with parts cobalt
in feldspathic glaze.
Height 24¾in (63cm).
Fired to 1220°C in
oxidation. By HANS DE
JONG (Holland), 1979.

Michael Casson (UK) often uses cut paper-resist in combination with incised drawing on pots where the decoration is inspired by landscape. The technique simply involves sticking cut shapes of newspaper on to leather-hard pots with a little water prior to dipping them into an iron-bearing slip and leaving them to dry. After removing the paper, which has prevented the slip from coating areas of the pot, further drawing can be cut through the slipped parts to complete the design, if not already done at an earlier stage. (Incising through one colour slip or oxide or glaze to reveal another colour underneath is known as 'sgraffito'.)

Stoneware bowl with paper-resist 'landscape' pattern and sgraffito through slip. $8\frac{1}{2} \times 5$in (21.6 × 14cm). Reduction fired. By MICHAEL CASSON (UK), 1982. In the author's collection.

BELOW: Three porcelain pots, with sgraffito pattern based on landscape. Height 10in (25.4cm) approx. By SHEILA CASSON (UK), 1982.

Unfired clay in the leather-hard state can be burnished to a shiny, reflective surface with smooth wooden, bone, metal or plastic tools. A spoon or a pebble work quite well. Red earthenware clays on a paler body, coated with a darker slip, are best suited to pieces on which a pattern is scratched in contrasting light, matt lines. **Siddig El'Nigoumi** (UK) is well-known particularly for his earthenware dishes decorated in this manner. Basically his dishes are circular, oval or rectangular shapes with rounded corners and gently sloping walls press-moulded from slabs of clay. He has a collection of differently shaped spoons and pebbles appropriately selected to fit various contours while burnishing the smooth Fremington clay he uses. Clays which are sandy in texture will also burnish well, but subsequent drawing is likely to be less crisp and even than with a really smooth body. Every one of his pieces carries a tiny, stylized drawing of a scorpion similar to symbols which he remembers seeing in the Sudan where he was born and which were intended "to ward off the evil eye".

When the dishes have been bisqued he places them upside-down on blocks of wood about 3 in. high to raise them clear of the ground. Then, with burning torches made from rolls of newspaper (much experiment has led him to believe that the *Daily Mirror* has the highest resin content and is most suitable for his purpose!), he directs the smoke and flame under and over the ware. To avoid the risk of cracking he does not allow dishes to become too hot, frequently wiping away soot from the surface to check the amount of carbonization that has taken place, until the desired result is achieved. This method, prompted through contemplating the variegated surface of an old Sudanese coffee-pot in his possession and noting the way in which smoke had affected it, can be controlled so that parts of the bisqued ware are blackened while other parts remain red. If several dishes are being treated with smoke, work can be continuous from one piece to another while allowing periods of cooling to occur naturally.

TOP RIGHT: Earthenware dish, press-moulded, burnished, incised and 'carbonised'. 10 × 9in (25.4 × 22.9cm). Fired to 800°C in an electric kiln and then smoked. By SIDDIG EL'NIGOUMI (UK), 1980.

RIGHT: SIDDIG EL'NIGOUMI [UK] incising one of his earthenware bowls which has been burnished prior to firing.

'Painted Slab'. Hand-built stoneware, blue-grey slip and copper oxide under white glazes, reduction fired to 1300°C in a gas kiln. Height 21⅝in (55cm). By GRAHAM BURR (UK), 1981.

Melted wax, a wax emulsion or a latex solution can be poured or painted on to the clay in both the dry and bisque states to act as a resist against oxides, stains, slips or glazes. The natural body colour then contrasts with the parts treated differently. Where certain glazes (such as those containing wood ash) are resisted on stoneware or porcelain bodies, the unglazed edges of the decoration are often stained orange with salts diffused outward from the glaze. Similarly, painted resists are used over slipped or stained areas usually under a white or light-coloured glaze. Bands of resist, precisely placed, make an important contribution to the tautly controlled form of the pot by **Ursula Scheid** (West Germany) left. For very sharp, straight-edge definition a commercial masking tape, such as is used in the automobile industry, makes an ideal resist material.

'Walzenvase'. Wheel-thrown porcelain, partly engobe under a feldspathic glaze, unglazed bands and rim (polished). Height 6½in (16.5cm). Fired in reduction to 1360°C. By URSULA SCHEID (West Germany), 1980.

ABOVE: Porcelain bowl, wheel-thrown, incised 'wave' pattern and carved rim fired in an electric kiln to 1280°C. Diameter 7½in (19cm). By PETER LANE (UK), 1981.

'Trees'. Bone china bowl, slip-cast in an engraved plaster mould (limited edition), unglazed. Height 3in (7.6cm) approx. Fired in an electric kiln to 1250°C. By PETER LANE (UK), 1980.

Relief carving has gained considerable popularity among those contemporary studio potters who wish to retain close control of the final surface appearance of their pieces. Porcelain potters, in particular, find their chosen material most amenable to incising, carving to varying depths within the wall thickness, or piercing to produce quite delicate fretwork. Clay bodies must be of extremely smooth, evenly consistent composition if they are to permit detailed carving. Individual craftsmen have their own preferences concerning the best conditions for cutting into the clay. I have found that I can obtain sharper definition when the piece has reached what might be described as a rather 'hard' leather-hard state. Moisture content is still evident, and this assists in the creation of clean lines free from burring, which occurs when the clay is too wet, and from the chipped edges that arise when it is too dry. The latter condition presents an extra hazard in the form of dust. Anyone scraping away at dry clay should *always* wear an effective face mask, to safeguard against the inhalation of silica particles and the risk of contracting silicosis. Open forms like bowls must be handed with great care, to judge the degree of pressure which may be applied, or fractures can occur which may

not be evident until the piece is fired. Much will depend upon relating the speed and pressure of the carving and piercing to the contours, thickness and condition of the form. The thinner the walls, the more gentle and sensitive the tooling should be.

ABOVE: 'Trees'. Porcelain bowl, thrown and carved, matt white glaze with pink lustred glaze. Dia. 10in (25.4cm). 1280°C oxidized. By PETER LANE (UK), 1980.

'Shell-edged Bowl'. Porcelain, thrown, with hand-formed individual flutes added to inside rim which is then pinched. Diameter 10½in (26cm). Barium glaze coloured pink fading into white. Fired in an electric kiln to Orton cone 10. By VIVIENNE FOLEY (UK), 1981.

ABOVE: Bowl, porcelain agate ware, press-moulded and carved. $3\frac{1}{2} \times 2\frac{3}{4}$in (8.9 × 7cm). Fired in an electric kiln to 1240°C. Colour has been added to the clay in the form of body stains and oxides prior to assembly. The piece is supported in a saggar to prevent distortion and collapse during firing. By DOROTHY FEIBLEMAN (UK), 1981.

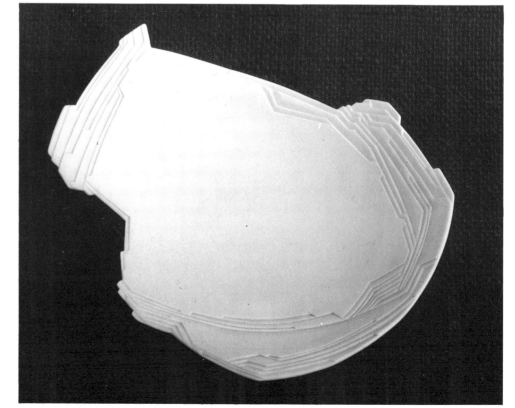

Porcelain bowl form with carved surface and rim by ALAN WHITTAKER (UK), 1982.

In addition to combining stained porcelains (described more fully in Chapter 5 on page 185) **Dorothy Feibleman** (UK) occasionally includes areas of finely carved fretwork in her pieces, painstakingly scraping away the bone-dry material. The slip-cast porcelain pieces by **Alan Whittaker** (UK), whose simple forms appear to be almost totally composed of dazzling filigree patterns, were produced by a quite different technique. The design is partially inscribed in the walls while leather-hard and finally completed, after firing until vitrified between 1230° and 1250°C, by directing silicon carbide grit (300–400 mesh at a pressure of about 180 psi) at the piece with a sand-blaster. Adhesive plastic tape protects parts which are to remain uncut. This process can be controlled so that the walls are either completely pierced or only a thin film of translucent material is retained in the recesses.

The extremely delicate and finely pierced or incised work of **Angela Verdon** (UK) is carried out with diamond-tipped drills on slip-cast, bone-china forms bisque fired to 1060°C. A lower bisque temperature leaves the body too soft to resist chipping and breaking, while a higher temperature hardens the bisque so that drilling becomes too difficult. Even at 1060°C the abrasive properties of the bisque soon blunt the drill tips. Finally, the pieces are fired to 1220°C in an electric kiln, and the intricate tracery becomes physically strong.

ABOVE RIGHT: Polished bone china form with incised and pierced surface, unglazed. Height 3½in (9cm). By ANGELA VERDON (UK), 1982.

RIGHT: Polished bone china form with pierced section (wall thickness is 1/10in) fired in an electric kiln (unglazed). Height 3¼in (8cm). By ANGELA VERDON (UK), 1982.

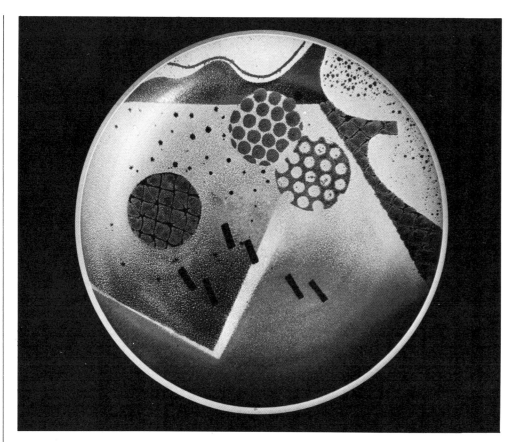

Porcelain platter, wheel-thrown with feldspathic glaze and various coloured slips sprayed over the basic glaze. Diameter 19½in (48.9cm). Glaze inlay and wax-resist techniques also used. Fired in reduction to Orton cone 11. By TIM MATHER (USA), 1982.

LEFT: Porcelain plate, semi-matt feldspathic glaze containing rutile, decorated by using cut and torn paper stencils and spraying coloured slips with iron, rutile and cobalt as colourants followed by wax-resist and further glaze dipping. Diameter 19½in (49.5cm). Fired to cone 11 in reduction. By TIM MATHER (USA), 1982.

Porcelain plate, with cut edge, black underglaze pencil drawing, pink stain airbrushed on rim, transparent glaze fired to cone 10 in oxidation. Gold lustre and red glass enamel then applied and plate re-fired to cone 018. Diameter 13in (33cm). By KEITH CAMPBELL (Canada), 1982.

The flowing lines and decorative motifs of **Keith Campbell's** (Canada) work reveal the influence of his interest in the Art Nouveau period. Working mostly on the wheel in series or limited editions, he makes thrown and press-moulded porcelain plates and shallow bowls using a metal rib to prepare a smooth, clean, hard surface for decorating.

'Cats' Whiskers'. Stoneware, thrown and hand-built, incised and painted decoration. Fired in oxidation to 1260°C. By MARIANNA FRANKEN (Holland), 1982.

Some of the finest relief carving on porcelain vessels is done by **Karl Scheid** (West Germany). The form and ornamentation of each of his pieces is carefully considered to ensure their precise and harmonious relationship. Such refined craftsmanship requires intense concentration throughout the whole process. The tools used are very simple: razor blades and loops of spring steel.

Anne Mercer (Australia) develops her ideas for modelled elements and incised motifs on porcelain from a variety of sources, but the carved insects which occupy the insides of some of her bowls began when she

ABOVE: Thrown, altered and incised porcelain bowl with celadon glaze. Height 4¾in (12cm), diameter 8¹¹⁄₁₆in (22cm). Heavily reduction fired between 1100° and 1300°C in a natural gas down-draught kiln. By ANNE MERCER (Australia), 1981.

RIGHT: Porcelain bowl, thrown and carved, with lime-feldspar glaze. Height 3¹⁵⁄₁₆in (10cm). Reduction fired to 1360°C. By KARL SCHEID (West Germany), 1981.

discovered a dead cockroach lying in a bowl. Since that moment, she has collected all kinds of 'bugs' to study as a basis for carved designs. Like many other potters working with relief carving, Anne Mercer relies on the type of glaze used initially by the Sung potters of China a thousand years ago to bring out the character of the drawing. Celadon glaze flows and accumulates in the depressions giving different tonal qualities according to depth and leaving the sharper edges to gleam through a thinner layer of glaze. **Scott Malcolm** (USA) cuts through as much as half the thickness of the pot wall when carving his detailed and often complex plant designs on porcelain under a celadon glaze. On closed bottle vases, where it is more difficult to judge the thickness of the wall, it is possible to cut too deeply and pierce the wall. He relates his pots to the contours of human form: "It's all hips, buttocks and breasts." He allows the thrown pieces to dry to the point when, no longer plastic, they can be handled without fear of distortion. The design to be carved is sketched on to the pot with a pencil (the graphite burns away in the kiln) to ensure that it fully complements the form. He leaves the kiln to cool for 48 hours following the glaze firing to reduce the risk of crazing the celadon.

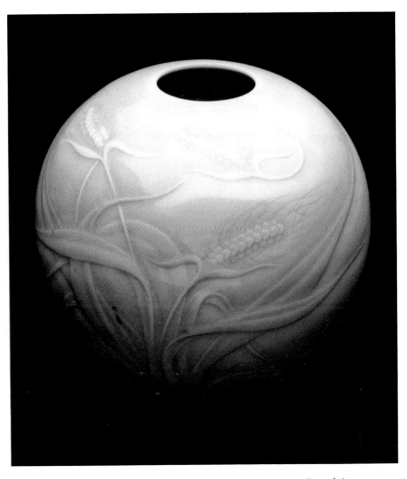

ABOVE: Porcelain vase, thrown and carved, with pale blue celadon glaze. Height 5½in (14cm). By SCOTT MALCOLM (USA), 1981.

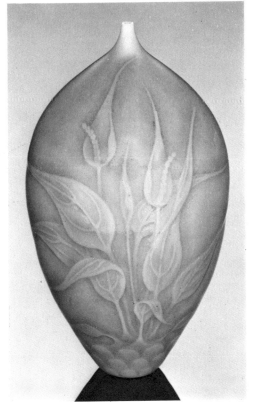

RIGHT: Small porcelain bottle, thrown and carved, 'spathaphyllium design', with green celadon glaze. Height 4½in (11.4cm). By SCOTT MALCOLM (USA), 1981.

ABOVE: 'Mountains, Clouds and Water'. Hand-built earthenware with painted oxides under a matt white glaze. Width 20in (55.9cm). Fired to 1100°C in an electric kiln. By TESSA FUCHS (UK), 1980.

Covered jar, stoneware, thrown, black slip surface with applied pink and blue squares. By BRUCE NUSKE (Australia), 1980.

A matt version of celadon glaze clothes the porcelain of some vases decorated with surface relief patterns by **Harlan House** (Canada). A very sharp metal loop tool, normally used for trimming, makes strong diagonal grooves as it 'chatters' across the almost dry surface of certain pieces.

RIGHT: 'Lonsdale Tobi Ganna Vase'. Thrown with 'chatter' marks, pale green matt celadon glaze. Height 8in (20.3cm). By HARLAN HOUSE (Canada), 1982.

ABOVE: Bottle vase, stoneware, engraved 'carp' design, off-white ash glaze. Height 15in (38cm) approx. Fired in reduction to 1300°C. By JIM MALONE (UK), 1981. In the collection of W. Ismay.

Hand-built stoneware form, coiled, wire-cut decoration applied and emphasized with iron and manganese oxides, matt black glaze. $13\frac{3}{4} \times 10\frac{1}{4}$in (35 × 26cm). Fired in oxidation to 1280°C. By HIROE SWEN (Australia), 1981.

ABOVE: Bowl, hand-built (slab) in fine red clay
with porcelain inlay, unglazed. Fired to cone 6.
By VIRGINIA CARTWRIGHT (USA), 1982.

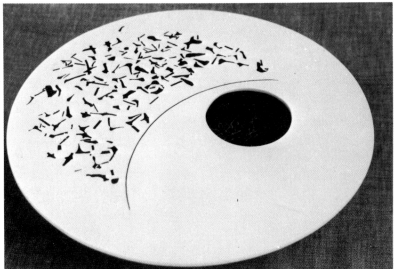

'After Kandinsky'. White earthenware, unglazed, slip-cast and assembled,
inlaid with black slip, inside glazed black. Height 4¾in (12cm), diameter 15in
(38cm). Fired in electric kiln to 1180°C. By LEO KING (New Zealand), 1981.

If pieces have very thick walls, layers can be removed and the whole surface deeply sculpted. **Nina Gaby** (USA) throws with a basic Grolleg body (55 parts Grolleg, 20 parts potash feldspar, 12 parts flint, 13 parts Pyrax, 3 parts bentonite), which has a fineness of grain, together with strength even at its thinnest points, giving her total freedom for carving. One series of carved pieces resulted from her fascination with the thickness of leaves of cacti and the imprints and holes present in them. Other influences come from lasting impressions formed while travelling in Europe: French Metro stations and other remnants of Art Nouveau; hours spent in the Victoria and Albert Museum sitting under Persian miniatures which encouraged her excitement for details; noticing rocks on beaches around Greek islands which helped her towards consideration of surface interest. Many of the potters with whom I have been in contact, and especially those who carve porcelain, acknowledge the influence of the Art Nouveau period upon their designs. In most cases they have no wish to reproduce even a flavour of that artistic style but similarities become almost inevitable. Certainly, decorative pieces are very much in vogue at the time of writing and we are sufficiently far removed from the period for fresh interpretations and approaches to be made. (It is interesting to note that the wallpaper designs and textile patterns of William Morris have also enjoyed a vigorous commercial revival in Britain since the 1960s.

Twisted strands of wire are often used for cutting thrown pots free from the wheelhead. If this wire is held taut and pulled beneath the base on a slowly revolving wheel it produces a distinctive raised, shell-like pattern. Slabs cut with such wire can be used for building textured pieces, and altering the movement, direction and speed of the pulling action can sculpt the surface in strong relief. The opposing slabs on either side of the cutting wire can be utilized, especially for positive/negative, male/female, interlocking faces or pieces. Slabs will stand alone quite easily without support if slightly bent or corrugated verti-

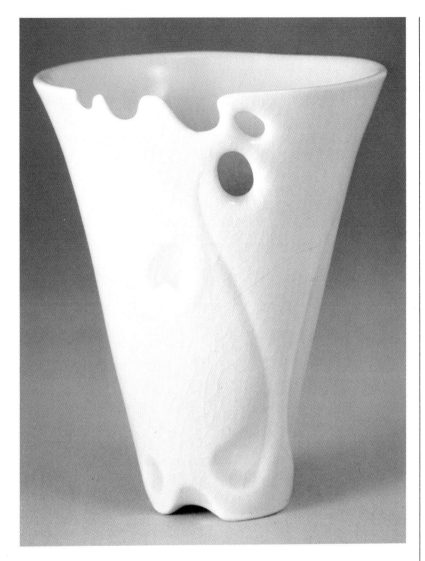

ABOVE RIGHT: Porcelain vase, thrown and carved, pale blue glaze. Height 4½in (11.4cm). Fired to cone 10 in oxidation. By NINA GABY (USA), 1979.

RIGHT: 'Bowl' raku form No. 466. Hand-built, hollow, unglazed. $16\frac{15}{16} \times 14\frac{15}{16} \times 11$in ($43 \times 38 \times 28$cm). By RICK RUDD (New Zealand), 1982.

cally. They can also be incorporated into wall panels or murals. Tightly wound spring wire, if not too thick a gauge, can be stretched and used to cut more exaggerated linear textures. Similar techniques form the basis of the sculptural and vessel forms featuring powerful, organized textures by both **Christa Gebhardt** and her husband **Johannes** (West Germany), although they work in their own individual and separate ways. Staining the recessed lines with oxides emphasizes the relief still further.

Figurine'. Stoneware, slab-built with relief-cut pattern, coloured slip under thin layer of matt glaze. Height $17\frac{11}{16}$in (45cm). Reduction fired to 1300°C. By CHRISTA GEBHARDT (West Germany), 1982.

Thrown and re-shaped stoneware form, feldspathic glaze with cobalt brushed on, followed by further layer of glaze containing rutile brushed on top. Height $18\frac{1}{8}$in (46cm). Fired in oxidation to 1280°C. By INGVIL HAVREVOLD (Norway), 1981.

RIGHT: 'Spoon'. Porcelain, thrown, turned and cut when leather-hard. Height 6½in (16cm). Ceramic pencil and underglaze colours under a clear matt glaze sprayed thinly. Fired in an electric kiln to 1260°C. By RUTH FRANKLIN (UK)

'Cap Form'. Porcelain, hand-built with inlaid coloured clays. Height 7½in (19.1cm), width 5½in (14cm). By MARIAN GAUNCE (UK), 1980.

ABOVE: 'Written Memory'. Slip-cast terracotta panel. $11\frac{13}{16} \times 21\frac{5}{8}$in ($30 \times 55$cm). Fired in oxidation to cone 08. By NINO CARUSO (Italy), 1980.

'Frog Jug'. Slip-cast in white earthenware, stained glazes. Height 8in (20.3cm). By TONY BENNETT (UK), 1980.

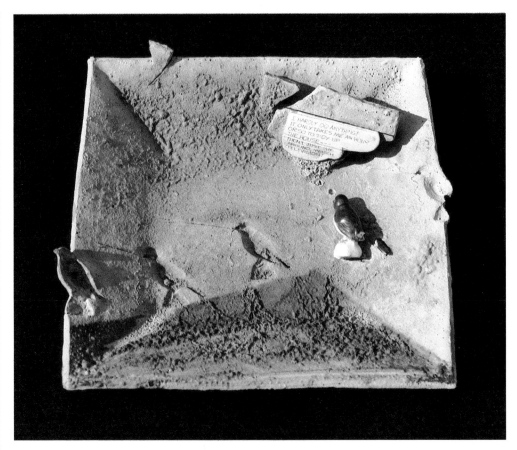

'An Average House-bird Stricken Guilty while Looking for a Piece of Tail'.. $14 \times 3 \times 3$in ($35 \times 7.6 \times 7.6$cm). Stoneware fired to cone 6 with cryolite glaze over manganese slip, followed by ceramic decals fired to cone 018. By JOHN CHALKE (Canada), 1980.

'Still Life with Pepper and Tomato'. Stoneware with slips and glaze. Width $13\frac{3}{4}$in (35cm). Fired to $1300°$C in reduction. By ANTJE BRUGGEMANN-BRECKWOLDT (West Germany), 1981.

5 COLOUR IN STUDIO CERAMICS

As a general, and perhaps rather loose, rule it is accepted that sculpted surfaces and complex structures in ceramic require finishing in monochrome, preferably with matt glazes or none at all. Discreet additions of different colours may be included provided that they do not distract attention from the overall concept. Immediately one makes this statement a host of images comes to mind pleading exception, mainly from the United States but also increasingly from elsewhere. Polychromatic treatments can undoubtedly fragment three-dimensional form. Different colours appear to advance or recede according to their particular juxtaposition, so that awareness of final colour and tonal relationships is an important factor in polychrome decoration. Since it is unlikely that the raw materials which provide the colours of the potter's palette will remain the same after firing, ceramic artists have to visualise final results as they work. Most potters aim to achieve a harmonious match between form and decoration, but some consciously use discordant colours in order to shock. Others reduce three-dimensional form to a subordinate role so that it acts merely as a supporting ground for graphic work, often of a quite sophisticated nature. Some may claim that their intent, their feeling, and the thought processes involved mark their work as 'fine art', while others are content merely to make 'decorative' objects. There are many whose approach to ceramics lies at other points in between. The number of variables presented by glaze composition, firing atmosphere and temperature, together with the colour response from oxides and fluxes, is infinite. Permutations of materials can be overwhelming, so that although potters may constantly prepare colour and glaze tests to fill empty corners of their kilns, most keep faith with a few glazes that they know well and whose behaviour they can accurately anticipate. Coloured slips are usually utterly predictable and have particular appeal to those who prefer not to use glaze at all.

Clay bodies can be deliberately coloured as a slip or in a plastic condition. This is done by adding percentages of metallic oxides or commercially prepared stains or, in some cases, a naturally darker clay, to a particular body and mixing thoroughly, in order to distribute the colour evenly. This is most easily accomplished in slips because the mixture can be put through a fine-lawn sieve for smooth dispersal with less risk of

OPPOSITE: 'Sphere'. Black porcelain/basalt body, unglazed, gold lustre application. By DEREK SMITH (Australia), 1981.

'Obelisk'. Stoneware, hand-built, inlaid slips and oxides. Height $25\frac{9}{16}$in(65cm). Fired in an electric kiln to 1240°C. By ANTOINE DE VINCK (Belgium).

speckling. Slip can, of course, be stiffened for use as a plastic body by draining in plaster moulds followed by wedging or pugging to the best possible condition. Lining the plaster moulds with nylon cloth prior to pouring the slips facilitates clean, easy removal once sufficient water has been drained off. Colour additions rarely exceed 15% and different shades or tones are achieved according to the proportions used.

Some potters prefer to add the stains as dry powder sandwiched between layered slabs of clay which are then kneaded thoroughly by hand. This tends to be less satisfactory than the slip preparation and specks of concentrated colour will, almost certainly, appear when fired. Such uneven colour may be used intentionally for textural variation. The dry material absorbs moisture from the clay, stiffening any with which it comes into contact and, for this reason, it is best added to fairly soft clay.

Dish, made from thrown elements, red body and one dark blue glaze (glass dust, barium carbonate, lithium, magnesium and clay), painted with several iron and copper glazes. Length 9⅞in(25cm). Fired in an electric kiln to cone 6a. By BEATE KUHN (West Germany), 1978.

Pedestal bowl, thrown and turned stoneware, 'T' material basalt body, with very dry 'cracked earth' glaze. Diameter 10½in(26.7cm). By GLYN HUGO (UK), 1982.

'Foreshore, Sea and Sky'. Slab-built pots, laminated and inlaid coloured stoneware. Height $10\frac{5}{8}$in(27cm) approx. By MICHAEL BAYLEY (UK), 1982.

Light-coloured clay bodies, especially white ones like porcelain, permit the purest colours. Heavy additions of oxide may alter the fluxing temperature of the body, but compatibility is most likely between stained and 'natural' portions of a piece if they are of the same basic composition. Successful mixtures and combinations of different bodies are a matter for experiment. The contrast of a coarsely textured iron-bearing body, such as a crank mixture, with a smooth porcelain, for example, has its own particular appeal exploited by numerous potters today. Fired to stoneware temperatures as inlays, marbled and agate wares, and so on, multicoloured ceramics produced from different or stained bodies are often left unglazed. A clear, transparent glaze does 'varnish' and brighten contrasting colours but often has

the disadvantage of possessing a highly reflective surface. On the other hand, a matt glaze tends to obscure the pattern.

Two commercially available clays are used by **Michael Bayley** (UK) for dishes and slab-built pots. Most of his work is based on natural form although man-made shapes sometimes appear in it. Landscape: mountains, trees, rocks, the seashore and skyscapes, are the main source of his ideas. His colours come from clays which fire to a dark chocolate and a light tan. Mixing the two together provides him with a mid-tone. Grog and sands are added to help resist warping and supply visual interest. The tonal textures and patterns are made by rolling the different coloured clays into one another. The striped patterns are produced by laminating different clays which are trimmed and knocked into blocks. From these, slices are taken to build the form or to be inlaid with other slabs through rolling. When completed the pots are once fired to 1280°C without glaze.

Johan Van Loon (Holland) uses a similar technique of rolling clays together but confines his work to ultra-thin stoneware with porcelain or coloured stoneware additions to make clearly defined patterns.

'Abstract'. Press-moulded, stoneware, laminated and inlaid clays, unglazed. Length 15¾in(40cm). Fired to 1280°C. By MICHAEL BAYLEY (UK), 1982.

BELOW: 'Elm Trees'. Inlaid coloured clays, stoneware slab, fired in oxidation (unglazed) to 1280°C. Height 16⅛in(41cm). By MICHAEL BAYLEY (UK), 1982.

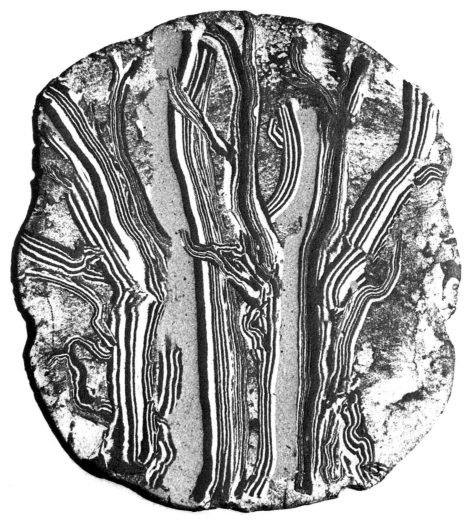

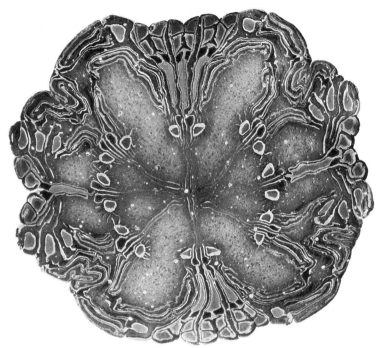

ABOVE: Coiled and beaten forms in grogged stoneware with iron, copper and sand on the surface and a hard, opaque feldspathic glaze poured on. By ROBERT FOURNIER (UK).

ABOVE RIGHT: Stoneware dish made from laminated coloured clays. Diameter $7\frac{1}{8}$in(18cm). The main colour is a mottled brown produced by the addition of copper carbonate to the body. Other colours include black, turquoise, coral and yellow produced from high percentages of body stains added to the clay. Once fired in an electric kiln to 1260°C. By MAL MAGSON (UK), 1980.

'Polka dot' bowl. Slabbed stoneware with white porcelain dots rolled in, shaped by pressing the slab round a cylinder. Diameter $9\frac{7}{16}$in(24cm). Transparent glaze inside, unglazed outside. Fired to 1200°C. By JOHAN VAN LOON (Holland), 1981.

Bowl, press-moulded from rolled-out slab of different coloured stoneware clays, glazed inside only with transparent glaze. Diameter $8\frac{1}{16}$in(20.5cm). Reduction fired to 1280°C. By JOHAN VAN LOON (Holland), 1981.

Separate pieces of coloured porcelain in the shape of florets, circles, spots, stripes, and so on, are rolled into a 'background' slab (which is itself sometimes coloured) for the cylindrical figures by **Jilly Ruhlman** (USA). These colourful objects could almost be mistaken for confectionery. Clear-glazed, they are later painted with lustres and enamels to detail facial features.

Porcelain is the chosen material of **Curt and Susan Benzle** (USA) because their work is concerned, they say, primarily with translucency and light, though colour is also an important consideration. Coloured elements within the forms heighten the dramatic interaction of light with translucent porcelain. A vessel which is blue on the inside and pink on the outside will respond with either a pink, a blue, or a mauve coloration, depending on the source and intensity of illumination. They feel that this endows the object with "a kinetic presence and vitality" not possible with opaque bodies. Colour is obtained with only four basic stains: yellow, pink, blue and black, which are mixed together for all other colour variations, in a body containing 40 parts feldspar, 30 parts china clay, 10 parts nepheline syenite and 10 parts flint. This is fired to 1270°C precisely. At this temperature the body begins to melt so, in most cases, additional support in the form of a cast saggar is provided. A transparent low-

ABOVE: Tumblers with butterfly and flower decoration, inlaid coloured porcelain, hand-built and fired to cone 9 in oxidation. Height 6in(15.3cm). By JILL RUHLMAN (USA), 1981.

'Spacewoman' vase. Hand-built with coloured porcelain, clear glazed, on-glaze enamel and lustre. Height 17in(43.2cm). By JILL RUHLMAN (USA), 1980.

'Redbank'. Hand-built porcelain with colour inlay. Diameter 7in(17.8cm). By CURTIS and SUZAN BENZLE (USA), 1982.

BELOW: Porcelain bowl form, hand-built with coloured inlay. Height 6in(15.2cm) approx. By CURTIS and SUZAN BENZLE (USA), 1982.

temperature glaze is usually applied after this and fired to cone 06. Bowl forms by the Benzles are constructed from anything between five and ten sections. These consist of slabs into which 'agate' slices of stained and layered clays have been rolled. Depending on the particular piece, trailed, inlaid or painted slip may be used in addition to incised and impressed patterning. Finally, the sections are placed in a mould, joined together and left to dry.

Porcelain pinched bowl with spiral decoration in white and coloured bodies under a shino glaze, fired in oxidation to 1260°C. By EWEN HENDERSON (UK), 1980.

'Sliced Agate'. Hand-built porcelain bowl. Diameter 6in(15.2cm). The translucency of the porcelain is intensified in the uncoloured ovals by the multicoloured haloes around them. Blue interior, green and metallic circles (painted oxides) under satin matt white glaze. Fired in an electric kiln to 1280°C. By MARY ROGERS (UK), 1980.

BELOW: Porcelain bowls constructed from individual slices of laminated, coloured clay ('agate') in blue and white. Diameter 4½in(11.4cm). Fired in an electric kiln. By DOROTHY FEIBLEMAN (UK), 1982.

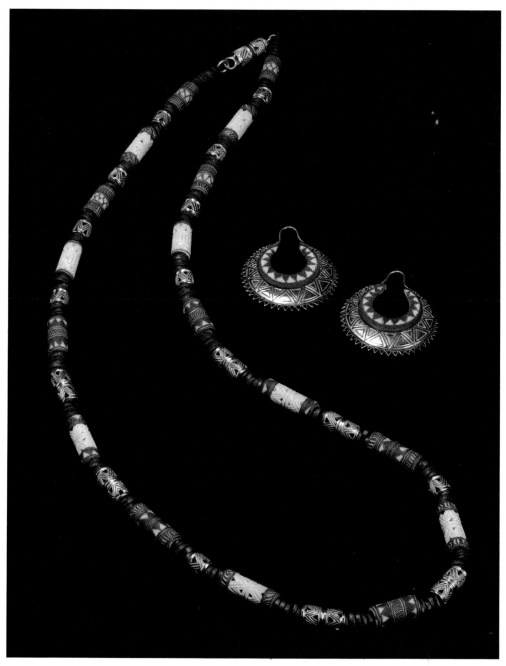

Porcelain necklace and earpieces, inlaid and carved coloured clays with painted gold lustre. By DOROTHY FEIBLEMAN (USA), 1982.

Extremely delicate, finely detailed agate ware of a high standard of design and craftsmanship is made by **Dorothy Feibleman** (UK). Her precise control in relating pattern and form endows her work with a jewel-like quality. She has evolved her own individual methods for constructing these pieces, but prepares her agate 'rods' in the traditional way. These consist of a central core or roll of porcelain clay around which coloured sheets of the same material, moistened with slip, are wrapped. Several layers may be added by this method to suit any combination of colour she has in mind. Thin slices can then be cut from the end of the roll ready for building the form. Differently shaped sections are made by squeezing and indenting the roll prior to slicing. The agate slices, of even thickness, are placed edge to edge with a little slip upon a sheet of white porcelain supported in a bisque-fired mould. This is allowed to dry bone-hard before being removed from the mould. She painstakingly scrapes away the white outer layer in order to reveal the agate design passing right through the wall. Such a bowl may take twenty hours to make and a high rate of loss during drying and firing has to be tolerated.

'Kimono'. Slab-built stoneware, incised design, painted with porcelain-based coloured slips. Height $17\frac{9}{16}$in(44.5cm). Fired to $1270°$C in an electric kiln. Black, white, sand and salmon colours. By JOHNNY ROLF (Holland), 1982.

Johnny Rolf (Holland) has produced her 'kimono' forms, using slabs prepared from a mixture of Dutch and German clays, sand and grog. The pieces are hollow but only a few inches deep. Since this particular shape is so closely associated with human form she feels that it "reflects the human torso and, through its decoration, creates an extension of the body". Decorative treatment consists of coloured porcelain-based slips and feldspathic glazes painted between a network of lines incised into the wet clay. Oxides are occasionally used to accentuate the linear grid. She believes that: "plants, animals and people all have their own nature, their own existence, but also a mutual, vulnerable relationship in the world they share. Travels to various parts of the world have deepened this insight, especially visits to pre-industrial cultures where the source of life seems nearer and more approachable." She tries to express some of these thoughts and feelings in ceramic terms.

RIGHT: Stoneware relief sculpture, slab-built, ash and feldspathic glazes, fired in oxidation to $1340°$C (cone 11). Height $12\frac{5}{8}$in(32cm). By DIETER CRUMBIEGEL (West Germany), 1978.

'Kimono'. Slab-built stoneware, painted with porcelain-based coloured slips. Height 19$\frac{11}{16}$in(50cm). Fired to 1270°C in an electric kiln. By JOHNNY ROLF (Holland), 1982.

BELOW RIGHT: 'Bust'. Hand-built porcelain with lustres. Fired to 1400°C. By MARIA KUCZYNSKA (Poland), 1982.

BELOW: 'Sitting Figure'. Hand-built, partly glazed porcelain with added lustre. Fired to 1400°C. By MARIA KUCZYNSKA (Poland), 1981.

Porcelain bowl with impressed texture and mottled glaze (brown/white) fired in reduction. By STIG LINDBERG (Sweden), 1979.

Robin Hopper (Canada) was originally trained as a printmaker and this probably accounts for his approach to colour in ceramics, and the presence of a modified two-dimensional feeling in some of his forms. Most of his work is in porcelain, chosen for its quality of whiteness which gives glazes more vibrant colour. Nature, landscape, geometry, ceramic history and ceramic chemistry are sources which mutu-

ally interact for him and they are interdependent. Nature or landscape often suggest the image; history or geometry the framework, and chemistry the methodology for his ceramics. He is fascinated by forgotten or seldom used techniques for surface enrichment, such as mocha-diffusion which he has thoroughly explored. In particular he draws sustenance from the ancient cultures of the Mediterranean and Mesopotamia,

'Krater'. Porcelain bowl with alkaline slip glaze containing copper and rutile, once fired. Height $7\frac{1}{16}$in(18cm). By ROBIN HOPPER (Canada), 1981.

Stoneware vase and bowl, decorated with porcelain slip under a tenmoku glaze fired in reduction. By STIG LINDBERG (Sweden), 1978.

especially Greek, Roman, Egyptian, Assyrian and Sumerian. A series of recent pieces clearly shows these influences in the forms, but the colours are more likely to have been suggested by Canadian landscape with its variations of tones and ever-changing effects of light. One of his 'dry' alkaline slip glazes is made up from 65% powdered porcelain body, 25% barium carbonate and 10% lithium carbonate. This is brushed on to 'green' (i.e. unfired) pots and then once fired. Colour is provided by copper carbonate which is applied as a spray,

and the pieces are fired in an electric kiln.

Visually interesting glaze textures can often animate quite ordinary forms. Two or more layers of different glazes will interact with each other to produce effects quite unlike anything which might be achieved from a mixture of the same glazes applied as one coat. If, in addition to colour potential, the characters of the glazes differ, variegated surfaces are more likely to result. For example, if a dry matt glaze is superimposed on to a fluid, shiny glaze, the outer surface will probably break and become mottled as the first layer melts. Other contrasts, such as light colours over dark ones (or the reverse), will emphasize the texture further. Similar use of glaze can be seen in the work of **Bryan Trueman** (Australia). His large stoneware platters give a broad expanse of flat surface that invites decorative glaze treatment. The methods employed by him include pouring, dipping, brushing, trailing, glaze sgraffito and wax-resist. Aspects of Australian and English landscape supply the impetus for his pictorial work. He fires the glost kiln quite rapidly (usually for four and a half hours) to 1100°C in an oxidising atmosphere. Once the glaze begins to melt he commences medium reduction. He holds this atmosphere and spends up to six hours between 1100°C and the maturing temperature of 1300°C, in order to smooth out the thickly applied glazes. When cone 10 falls the kiln is 'soaked', continuing the reduction atmosphere, for about thirty minutes, at which point damper and burner ports are all sealed and slow cooling begins. The four main glazes used are a tenmoku, a chun, a titanium-based, and a copper-red glaze.

'Baroque Bowl'. Stoneware, thrown and altered with 'pulled' additions. Height 5½in(14cm), diameter 11 9/16 in(30cm). Chun glaze over saturated iron-red glaze, reduction fired to Orton cone 9. By IAN FIRTH (New Zealand), 1982.

Large stoneware platter, thrown, painted with tenmoku and titanium glazes to depict landscape with trees. Diameter 16½in(42cm) approx. By BRYAN TRUEMAN (Australia), 1981.

'Nang' a (Grape-vine)', porcelain lidded bowl with brushwork design. Height 6in(15.2cm), diameter 13in(33cm). Reduction fired to cone 9. By JOHN TAKEHARA (USA), 1981.

BELOW: Porcelain plate with trailed and brushed coloured glazes on transparent glaze. Diameter 17in(43.2cm). Reduction fired. By CATHERINE HIERSOUX (USA), 1982.

Porcelain plate with underglaze crayon drawing in black, clear-glazed and fired to cone 10 in oxidation. Diameter 13in(33cm). Orange and gold lustre applied and fired to cone 018. By KEITH CAMPBELL (Canada), 1981.

Catherine Hiersoux (USA) uses rubber syringes to trail a matt grey glaze, a white glaze and a tenmoku on top of a transparent porcelain glaze, working from light to dark. The trailed designs are trimmed and shaped when dry to define and control the flow as they melt in the kiln. Patterns tend to occupy the central area of her thrown porcelain plates in an asymmetric and seemingly casual way, yet there is considerable colour and tonal subtely. Catherine Hiersoux's tall, columnar pots are sprayed with multiple glazes, and each successive layer is fired before the next is added.

Square porcelain plate, press-moulded with seven overlapping coloured glazes (poured). Width 13½in(34.3cm). By SYLVIA HYMAN (USA), 1982.

Rectangular stoneware dinner plates, trapezoidal, triangular and square serving platters, and bowls made by **Sylvia Hyman** (USA) are dipped in at least four different glazes. Masking tape is used to define clear edges when dipping in glaze tanks which she has constructed from sheets of Plexiglass to accommodate plates and dishes up to 22 in. wide. Matt and glossy, light and dark layered glazes produce both bright and subtle hues on the same object. "Interesting things happen where glazes of different composition and melting points overlap each other."

Layering glazes by pouring and trailing methods leaves much to chance because it is virtually impossible to gauge exact thicknesses which are built up. The porosity of the bisqued ware is an important factor here together with the composition of the glazes. A high proportion of clay in a glaze will increase the shrinkage rate as it dries, causing the surface to develop a network of cracks. In some cases this problem, which could lead to glaze cracking in the kiln, can be alleviated by gently rubbing a finger across the dry glaze so that the powdery material is smoothed over to fill the cracks. Where the thickness of glaze is too great there is further risk that parts may flake off when they dry or if the pot is handled carelessly. There may be other occasions when cracking is consciously encouraged to form part of the decoration, and thick applications of glaze with a high clay content will ensure that this takes place. Adhesion to the pot is threatened when one glaze is poured too thickly over another but, as with so many techniques, constantly widening experience develops sensitivity and judgement to the point where the work be-

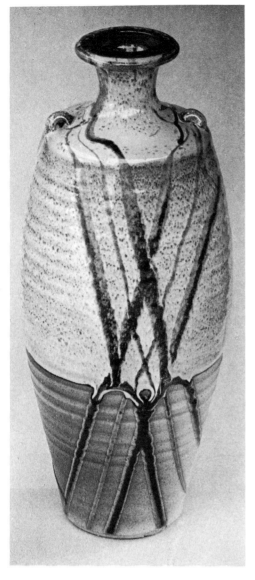

Covered jar, stoneware with rich tenmoku glaze, iron oxide brushwork, and red, pink and blue glaze painting. Height $7\frac{1}{16}$in(18cm). Reduction fired. By DAVID EELES (UK), 1981. In the author's collection.

LEFT: Stoneware vase, slipped to halfway in thin tomato-red glaze with thick soda chun glaze dipped over. A copper-red glaze is then trailed on top. Height 18in(45.7cm). Wood fired. By DAVID EELES (UK), 1982.

comes instinctive. Personal variations of familiar, traditional methods abound. **David Eeles** (UK), for example, uses a multiple trailer which he made from a thrown pot to which he has attached a group of nozzles or spouts of different diameters for pouring glaze. The speed and directional movement of such a tool in use offers considerable scope for anyone with imagination, especially where large areas are available for decoration. The late **Shoji Hamada** (Japan) used to ladle a pattern of glazes trailed across large, previously glazed (unfired) dishes in a delightfully free and spontaneous manner to great effect.

RIGHT: Stoneware plate, thrown, various glazes and pigments brushed and trailed. Diameter 15in(38.1cm). Reduction fired to 1280°C. By DAVID EELES (UK), 1982.

ABOVE: Stoneware teapot, with iron brushwork, reduction fired to 1300°C. By DAVID LEACH (UK).

RIGHT: Stoneware bottles with rust-red (iron) decoration on tenmoku glaze, reduction fired. By DAVID LEACH (UK).

BELOW RIGHT: Coil-built pot with black matt and cobalt matt glazes and latex-resist design. $15\frac{3}{4} \times 14\frac{1}{8}$in($40 \times 36$cm). Fired in an electric kiln to 1280°C. By HIROE SWEN (Australia), 1981.

BELOW: Stoneware vase, underglaze brushwork (red iron oxide and clay mixed) over white-slipped surface. Height $3\frac{1}{4}$in(8.3cm). Reduction fired to 1300°C. By HENRY HAMMOND (UK).

Vessel form, hand-built earthenware with sgraffito design cut through purple-black glaze on top of fired white tin glaze. 20 × 15in(55.9 × 38.1cm). Fired in oxidation. By JAMES TOWER (UK), 1979.

Separàtely applied glaze layers also feature in the work of **James Tower** (UK) but the process involved is quite different. Every piece is pressmoulded in earthenware clay which fires to a pale buff colour at 1100°C. Following the normal bisque firing, the forms are covered with a white tin glaze and re-fired before being glazed again with a dark colour on top of the white. James Tower may sometimes subject a piece to four or five firings until the result satisfies him. Prior to re-firing the second (dark) glaze he scratches through this friable coating to expose the white beneath. This technique allows the potter more precise control over the surface pattern because the second glaze layer is of a reasonably consistent thickness. Many of his pieces reflect his interest in natural phenomena but now and then geometric decoration is used. A particular fascination for him is the element of movement and rhythm expressed with, and against, the form. This seems to him to be an essential ingredient which is often difficult to achieve. "To be successful it has to be a total and complete interrelation of form and decoration." James Tower is one of the relatively few British potters/ceramic sculptors whose work has regularly been exhibited in an established London gallery (Gimpel Fils) which is normally committed to showing fine art – the popular definition of which usually excludes contemporary ceramics.

White tin glaze provides an excellent ground for subsequent colour additions in both earthenware and stoneware if the potter wishes to prevent intrusion of body colour from the clay. **Hans de Jong** (Holland) recently abandoned his use of sgraffito techniques, for which he is well-known, in favour of exploring glaze overlays. He covers bisqued forms with a heavy layer of white tin glaze, applies coloured glazes over this and finally covers the whole with a transparent glaze before firing to 1220°C in an oxidizing atmosphere. He aims to intensify the relationship of the inside and outside of a form by organizing colour and decoration with glazes.

Rich glaze colours and textures have been a strong feature of the work of German potters for many years. It is a tradition that continues to hold firm despite the advent of much sculptural work. I have heard a number of British potters describe some of the German ceramics as 'overglazed' in the sense that reliance upon glaze is too heavy; as if a kind of 'overkill' treatment has been given to indifferent forms. There are several shades of opinion on this aspect but it cannot be denied that enviable glazes have been developed by German potters. Certainly **Margarete Schott** (West Germany) and **Hildegard Storr-Britz** (West Germany) are just two of those whose richly varied surfaces are widely admired. Multiple glaze layers and brushed oxides in such skilled hands produce depths of colour that suggest looking into, rather than at, the surface. Margarete Schott searches for unusual glaze ingredients and enjoys experimenting with them, firing up to 1360°C in her gas kiln under reducing conditions.

'Polder'. Slab-built stoneware plate with tin glaze and feldspathic glaze stained with oxides, with transparent majolica overglaze. Width $13\frac{3}{4}$in(35cm). Fired to 1220°C in oxidation. By HANS DE JONG (Holland), 1982.

'Tapered Slab: Painted Grid'. Stoneware, slab-built. $17\frac{1}{8} \times 15\frac{1}{8} \times 3\frac{3}{4}$in ($43.5 \times 38.5 \times 9.5$cm). Blue-grey slip and copper oxide under white glaze. Reduction fired to 1300°C. By GRAHAM BURR (UK), 1981.

Stoneware bottle with mineral glaze containing iron oxide and some additional iron oxide brushed on. Height 8⅝in(22cm). Reduction fired to 1360°C. By MARGARETE SCHOTT (West Germany), 1981.

ABOVE: Oval bowl, porcelain with feldspathic glaze fired in reduction to 1250°C.
$3\frac{15}{16} \times 6\frac{1}{2} \times 5\frac{5}{16}$ in(10 × 16.5 × 13.5 cm)
. By HILDEGARD STORR-BRITZ and JAMES STORR (West Germany), 1976.

'Glaze Painting'. Multiple glazes trailed and painted on grey feldspathic glaze, reduction-fired stoneware, 1250°C in a gas kiln. By HILDEGARD STORR-BRITZ and JAMES STORR (West Germany), 1980. In collection of Keramik Museum, Höhr-Grenzhausen.

Hildegard Storr-Britz's preference is for using the decorative potential of glazes on tile panels. Some of the tiles were cut from rolled clay slabs which were then bisque fired after a very slow drying period to prevent warping. Alternatively, she uses kiln shelves (bats), readily available from suppliers of pottery materials. Glaze painting is carried out on these flat surfaces with brushes and syringes in a direct way. Slow firing is essential to 500°C (maturing temperature 1250°C–1280°C) and cooling down must be very gradual between 800° and 100°C.

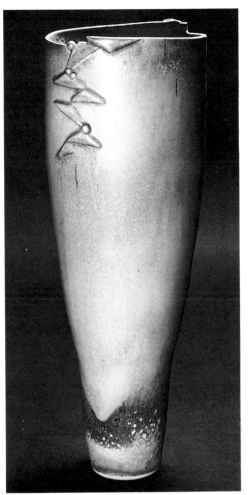

ABOVE: Thrown and hand-built stoneware form with variegated green crystal glaze. Height $7\frac{1}{16}$in(18cm). Fired in oxidation to 1280°C. By INGVIL HAVREVOLD (Norway), 1981.

LEFT: 'Edge-scape Vessel'. Porcelain, hand-thrown in sections and assembled. Height $16\frac{1}{4}$in(41.3cm). Crystalline matt glaze fired to Orton cone 11. By SALLY BOWEN PRANGE (USA), 1981.

RIGHT: Porcelain vases, formed around a cylinder. Beaten, applied and incised decoration, with copper oxide under celadon glaze. Height $3\frac{15}{16}$in(10cm). Fired in reduction to 1300°C, (tinged red and green from the copper reduction). By ROSEMARIE BRITTAIN (New Zealand), 1979.

Crystalline glazes with their somewhat flamboyant and unpredictable results present a challenge for many potters. A few do use such glazes consistently, although for others they may have no more than novelty interest. Their popularity is mercurial. Semi-matt, crystal glazes have a less overpowering presence than glossy ones in which large crystals are more likely to predominate. Low percentages of alumina are present in crystalline glaze composition and, without the stiffening property of this material, glazes are inclined to run, especially on smooth porcelain. In this case, pots are usually elevated on cylinders placed in a shallow dish or on a bat to protect the kiln shelf from glaze drips.

Diane Creber (Canada) is one potter who specializes in crystalline glaze for her one-off pieces. She experimented with many different formulas and firing procedures before settling on the one basic recipe she uses now for her 'white crystal' glaze:

Ferro frit 3110	48.4
Zinc oxide	24.4
Kaolin	1.5
Silica	17.9
Titanium dioxide	7.8
	100.0

(This was originally obtained by her from *Ceramics Monthly* December 1975, but she does not find it necessary to calcine either the alumina or zinc oxide.)

Blue crystals on a white-to-tan background are obtained by adding between 0.5% and 1% cobalt carbonate to the above. Green crystals come from an addition of between 1% and 4% copper carbonate to the base glaze, and tan crystals from between 1% and 3% manganese dioxide. Other oxides Diane Creber uses to a lesser degree are nickel oxide, uranium oxide and a vanadium stain. Interesting results occur when two or more of these are mixed together. A thicker than normal application of glaze is brushed on in several coats because some of the glaze runs off during firing. She stands the glazed porcelain pot on a pedestal, made from the same body, that matches the diameter of the foot. Glue, mixed with a little alumina, sticks the bisqued pot and pedestal together as they stand in a bisqued stoneware bowl which will hold the overflow of glaze. Due to the fluid nature of the glaze it is only used on the exterior. The kiln is fired as quickly as possible to cone 9. At this point, the kiln is switched off, the door opened and all bungs removed to cool it quickly to 1120°C. When this temperature is reached the door is closed, the kiln resealed and burners re-ignited. The temperature is allowed to drop a further 65°C approximately over the next six hours. For accurate readings of air temperature inside the chamber during this period, Diane Creber uses a voltmeter which gives a digital read-out of the number of mini-volts signalled from the thermocouple. This is translated into degrees Celsius with the aid of a conversion scale. Below 1010°C the crystals are frozen, so the kiln is switched off when this temperature is reached, and allowed to cool naturally.

Variations in crystal shapes can be achieved by holding the temperature for longer around 1095°C or in the cooler range of 1025°C. Smaller sized crystals occur when

the kiln is 'soaked' for a shorter period of time. A diamond-tipped glass cutter is used to score round the junction of the pedestal and foot-ring. A titanium-tipped chisel is then tapped around the scored line until the pot breaks away. Finally, the bottom is well-ground on a silicon carbide grinding wheel until completely smooth.

Porcelain bottle, with white crystal glaze. Height 10½in (26cm). By DIANE CREBER (Canada), 1982.

Agate bottle and bowl, white porcelain thrown with small addition of black-stained porcelain, turned, fired to 1250°C in an electric kiln and polished. Height of bottle $5\frac{15}{16}$in(15cm). By JOHN PARKER (New Zealand), 1982.

Buff stoneware bottle, incised pattern with iron oxide rubbed in and wiped off the surface. Height 6in(15.2cm). Dry matt glaze. Reduction fired to 1290°C. By CHRISTINE BALL (Australia), 1980.

'Guinea Fowl'. Hand-built stoneware, incised, with painted glazes. Height 8in(20.4cm) approx. By ROSEMARY WREN and PETER CROTTY (UK), 1982.

Extremely dry glazes containing large percentages of china clay offer good colour response in total contrast to the above. Their non-reflective surfaces are ideally suited to sculptural objects, such as the animal and bird forms made by **Rosemary Wren and Peter Crotty** (UK), who work together at the Oxshott Pottery in Devon. They use a white, high clay, matt glaze fired to 1265°C in an updraught propane gas kiln. This base glaze is coloured by adding oxides for yellows and blues. (A dark celadon glaze provides the green, and textured browns are obtained when used over an iron oxide wash.) Neat cobalt oxide gives black; iron oxide provides the rust-red; while chrome oxide supplies a drier green. These colours are laboriously painted on bisqued ware in patterns delineated by incised lines drawn into the surface at the leather-hard state. Unlike direct decoration on bisque ware alone without prior preparation, "incising the clay allows infinite readjustment of colour-shapes to fit the form – and of form to fit the pattern".

Traditional English slipware is rather less in evidence than it was only a few years ago but a number of British studio potters still favour the slip-trailing technique for decorating production wares and also individual pieces, notably dishes or large platters. The fluid nature of this process does not, in itself, seem to encourage the exploration of imagery far removed from the familiar designs of the seventeenth and eighteenth centuries. Colours, likewise, still tend to be mainly browns, blacks and whites under a very shiny glaze. Vibrant colours have become much more familiar in studio ceramics during the last decade. With the revival of interest in the possibilities offered by the earthenware medium, this trend seems likely to continue.

Earthenware dish with slip-trailed decoration in black, white, green and brown. Diameter 20in(55.9cm). Fired to 1100°C in an electric kiln. By JOHN POLLEX (UK), 1982.

GODFREY ARNISON (UK) trailing slip on an earthenware dish at the leather-hard stage. The dish is thrown in terracotta clay, and white slip is poured on the top surface. The design has been roughly marked out using a brush and watercolour paint which burns away in the firing, 1981.

Round comma-shaped bowl in high-fired red earthenware, with inlaid clays, part-glazed with white-turquoise glaze and enamel colours. By JACQUELINE PONCELET (UK), 1981.

Hand-built earthenware jug with painted decoration. Height 12$\frac{3}{16}$in(31cm). By ALISON BRITTON (UK), 1979. In the Crafts Council Collection.

Colours of remarkable brilliance have been favoured by potters such as **Greg Daly** (Australia) and **John Parker** (New Zealand), the former working with earthenware glazes and the latter with porcelain. Brilliant shades of blue and purple on some of Greg Daly's pieces are produced from copper carbonate in an alkaline glaze fired in an electric kiln between 1000° and 1100°C. He points out that a wide range of colour can be obtained with three variables: the proportion of barium carbonate; thickness of glaze; and, most important, temperature ("a difference of 10°C will affect the glaze. In 50°C colours will range from a dry purple to a satin cobalt blue"). Here are a few sample recipes:

	Light blue	Purple to dark blue	
Nepheline syenite	55	19	
Barium carbonate	26	40	
Lithium carbonate	2	5	1000°C
Flint	7	10	1100°C
China clay	6	19	
Copper carbonate	4	7	

RIGHT: Vase, oxidised stoneware, hand-built, painted with coloured slips. Height 6⅞in(17.5cm). By ELIZABETH FRITSCH (UK), 1979. In the Crafts Council Collection.

Earthenware form, thrown, slip-painted, and cut while the clay is soft. Height 11 9/16 in(30cm). By VILMA HENKELMAN (Holland), 1982.

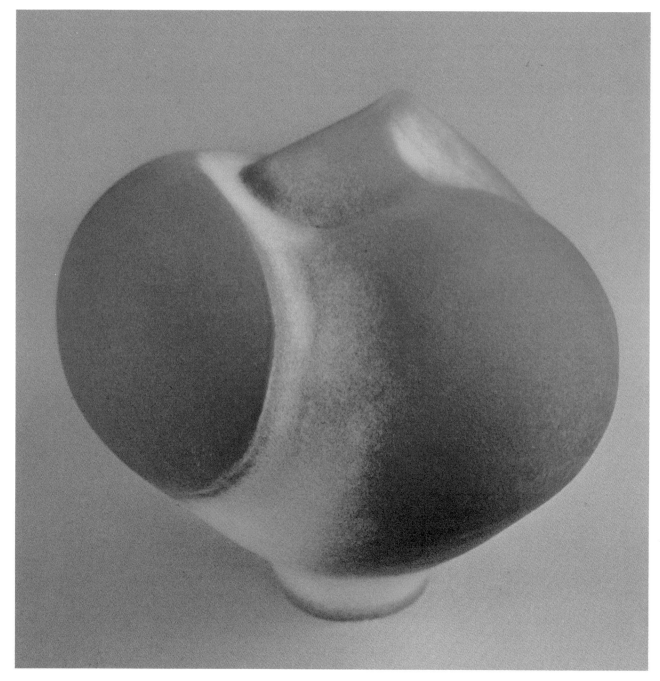

Bright colours from low-fired (750°C) on-glaze enamels and lustres applied by brush, or in the form of decals, have also become increasingly popular. In normal use these are applied on a pre-fired glaze. White or light-coloured glazes provide the most suitable background on which to display colour and detail. Few potters make their own lustres because more reliable commercial products are readily available. **Erik Gronborg** (USA) believes that the decoration "is at least seventy-five per cent of the artistic accomplishment of any work of

Thrown, 'expanded' and beaten earthenware form, with sprayed barium/lithium/copper glaze, fired to 1060°C in an electric kiln. Height 13in(33cm). By GREG DALY (Australia), 1981.

ceramics". He sees his own work in porcelain as being related to the traditions of eighteenth and nineteenth-century Europe, with the emphasis on "fragile delicacy, brilliant colours in lustres, and elaborate decoration". But he also uses all the means of expression which he feels are characteristic of today. In addition to moulds and stamps he uses photographic transfer techniques because "they produce effects typical of a modern industrial society: perfectly mechanical repetition of a form, shapes based seemingly on engineering logic rather than art history, just like automobiles on an assembly line". He uses photography in his work rather than drawing and painting because "the photograph is the most overwhelming means of visual communication: newspaper photographs, magazine advertizing, television. To most people a photograph still has some sense of being the objective 'real' world in a way that drawings have not". He makes his own photographic decals so that he can choose and control the images. These are all made in black and white to preserve the traditional relationship to photography and the colours are painted on later.

ABOVE: The two red pots are bisqued to 1200°C and re-fired to 1060°C in an electric kiln, with commercially prepared glaze. Height of blue bottle 8in(20cm) which is made in porcelain fired to 1250°C in an electric kiln, with barium matt glaze stained with cobalt. The glaze reveals 'islands' of crystals in parts. By JOHN PARKER (New Zealand), 1982.

Porcelain plate with photographic decals and lustre decoration. 20 × 21in(50.8 × 53.4cm). By ERIK GRONBORG (USA).

OPPOSITE: Stoneware form with 22 carat gold lustre and etched surface. Height 19$\frac{11}{16}$in(50cm). By ALAN PEASCOD (Australia), 1981.

RIGHT: Earthenware plate, chocolate-coloured body, central area has white semi-matt glaze with incised design and painted gold and silver lustres. Diameter 11in(28cm) approx. By JOHN CHIPPERFIELD (UK), 1974. In the author's collection.

BELOW RIGHT: Porcelain pot, thrown and turned, on-glaze lustre decoration. Height 4$\frac{1}{2}$in(11.5cm). By GEOFFREY SWINDELL (UK), 1980.

Low-fired lustres for oxidizing atmospheres consist of metallic salts, mixed with combustible resin and oils that burn away in the kiln, to deposit a bright film of metal or iridescent colour on the glazed surface. They are at their best when thinly applied to a glossy surface, offering richly colourful effects, as can be seen in the work of **Geoffrey Swindell** (UK).

Alan Peascod (Australia) prefers to work with lustres which he prepares himself for firing on to stoneware or porcellaneous bodies which have been glazed with 50 parts nepheline syenite; 25 parts silica; 25 parts frit, 3110 or equivalent; a part kaolin to a temperature between 1220° and 1250°C. He has discovered that a more metallic appearance is sometimes obtained when lustres are applied to a very thin layer of this glaze. After much experiment, he decided that he could use the same pigment recipes on both low and high-fired glazes and that lower oxide content was necessary with really efficient control over the reducing atmosphere. He prepares his pigments from powdered terracotta clay or burnt umber and oxides (dry) and grinds the mixture into a thick paste with water and acetic acid. Ruby reds, purples, silver and gold within his palette come from varying the proportion of copper oxide or copper carbonate, silver nitrate and bismuth oxide in relation

Bowl, tin-glazed earthenware. 12 × 3½in (30.5 × 8.9cm). Painted in iron-brown, dilute manganese, and manganese-cobalt black on tin glaze containing titanium, which emphasizes the iron colours. Wood firing deepens the iron colour and speckles the glaze near the rim due to light reduction in firing. By ALAN CAIGER-SMITH (UK), 1980.

to a set amount (approximately two-thirds parts by weight) of terracotta clay in the recipe. The pigments may be trailed, brushed on, or used with wax-resist or sgraffito techniques. When storing pigments containing silver nitrate it should be remembered that this is sensitive to light and it will undergo chemical change unless stored in a dark cupboard. Firing these pigments in his 30 cu. ft ceramic fibre kiln, Alan Peascod has found that 640°C is the optimum temperature for the reduction to begin. The kiln is held at this temperature until draw trials indicate that the reduction has produced satisfactory results (perhaps after an hour or more). Then the kiln is allowed to cool in a natural oxidizing atmosphere. Finally, the pots are scrubbed under water to clean away the clay pigment and reveal the lustre beneath. (For fuller details of these processes refer to *Pottery in Australia* Vol. 20 No, 1, May/June 1981.)

The superb lustres produced at the Aldermaston Pottery in Hampshire by **Alan Caiger-Smith** (UK) are widely acclaimed. A 160 cu. ft wood-fired kiln is taken to, and

maintained at, around 660°C, when alternating periods of reduction and oxidation begin for an hour or so until the colours have matured. He uses pigments containing lead and alkaline frits and about 70% ochre on top of the pre-fired (1060°C) tin-glazed earthenware. Ground pumice and raw sheep's wool is used to remove the pigment from the fired lustre. The red Fremington clay (from north Devon) from which Alan Caiger-Smith makes his lustre and other tin-glazed wares seems to add a warm glow to what could otherwise be a rather cold and dead white. Fluent brush strokes, with oxides directly painted or applied over wax-resist, cover the surfaces with bold calligraphic patterns. Unlike early majolica, which was painted on to bisqued pots under the glaze, Alan Caiger-Smith also uses the more difficult technique of painting over the unfired powdery glaze surface. Copper (green), cobalt (blue), iron (reddish-brown), vanadium (yellow), manganese (plum brown), chrome (dull green and pinks to reds), are the main sources of colour, and these oxides can be intermixed to modify or give greater variety to the potter's palette.

A special interest of **Eric James Mellon** (UK) has been the development of his own ash glazes for stoneware and, occasionally, for porcelain, under which he paints his distinctive figure compositions (often based on classical mythology) with colouring oxides. Every time he decorates a bowl he is attempting "to explain and enhance" the thrown form "by using the only means open to the artist; that is by using lines, and once the line joins up it becomes a shape; and when this is filled in it becomes an area. The careful understanding and use of these three things create a world of visual surprise, excitement and aesthetic delight". He likes pot shapes to be positive: "straight cylinders, well-proportioned bowls with good rims and feet, and rounded, bulbous shapes like onions". Many different wood ashes are used, such as pine, beech, willow, elm, apple, pear, cypress, chestnut, blackcurrant, and so on, for glazes that will give the best possible colour response both in range and density. He decorates both the inside and outside surfaces of many of his bowls mainly in buffs, browns, earthy reds, blues and greens of a subtle nature and subdued in tone. The colours, varying according to the overglaze, come mainly from iron, cobalt and chromium oxides fired in an electric kiln.

ABOVE: Covered jar, painted with copper-red lustre on tin glaze, and reduced in third firing for lustre after normal bisque and glost firings. Height 13in(33cm). By ALAN CAIGER-SMITH (UK).

Bowl, stoneware with philadelphus ash glaze. Diameter 13½in(34.3cm). Painted decoration depicts 'Persephone reclining with a reflection in a mirror and entertained by musicians, Ascalaphus (the owl), a cat and butterflies'. By ERIC JAMES MELLON (UK).

Sandra Taylor (Australia) finds subject matter for her sculptural pieces and decorated plates from among the birds, animals, plants and people observed in the environs of Sydney where she lives. Her colourful, amusing and sometimes satirical imagery is created with painted oxides and inlaid coloured clays.

'Sydney Beach Scene: Lady Jayne'. Stoneware with oxides, underglaze stains and inlaid coloured clays under matt and glossy glazes and on-glaze painting. Width 18⅞in(48cm), height 15in(38cm), depth 15in(38cm). The potter tells us: "Lady Jayne is a nudist beach – notorious as a homosexual pick-up spot. The beach is often empty. People prefer to acquaint themselves behind rocks or in the water where they are afforded some privacy. I have taken my view of the beach from the water looking in, as the beach has become a weekend tourist attraction for boat-owners". By SANDRA TAYLOR (Australia), 1981.

ABOVE: Covered jar, wood-fired stoneware.
Height 14in(35.5cm). By KAREN KARNES (USA),
1982.

Lidded jar, stoneware with banded oxides,
wood fired. Height 14in(35.6cm). By KAREN
KARNES (USA), 1980.

Heavy concentrations of metallic oxides are inclined to run at high temperatures, whether applied under or over a glaze, and the colour is likely to be very dark to matt black. This fluxing property is used to good effect by potters who paint bands of oxides on to their pots – especially around the rims of bowls. Random dribbles of colour run down the walls according to the weight of oxide used and the character of the glaze. **Emmanuel Cooper** (UK) often applies oxides to the rims of his porcelain bowls. He wants his pieces to "relate to the space they occupy as well as the space around them". He is not interested in attempting to exploit the translucent property of the porcelain body nor to make his pieces with eggshell-thin walls, but "the pots have to feel good when handled".

A mixture of copper and manganese oxides brushed heavily on to clay, particularly porcelain, fluxes to a brassy appearance without the use of glaze. Perhaps the best exponent of this technique is **Lucie Rie** (UK) who completes all her pieces in the 'green' state prior to firing direct to 1250°C in an electric kiln. Horizontal bands of brushed oxides are often used by her to emphasize and complement directional changes of profile, especially in tall-necked bottle vases. Vertical or diagonal lines may be scratched through the oxide very pre-

ABOVE: Porcelain bowl, green, speckled glaze with black and gold pigment on rim. Fired to 1260°C in an electric kiln. By EMMANUEL COOPER (UK), 1982.

Stoneware form with dry ash glaze poured in varying thicknesses. By SHEILA FOURNIER (UK).

cisely to reveal the white body underneath. Another method she uses is to brush oxides over and into cross-hatched incised linear banding. The top surface is then carefully cleaned with a damp sponge to pick out the pattern of lines inlaid with oxides. When covered with a semi-matt white glaze (also applied by brush at this stage), traces of copper bleed out from these lines and tint the glaze with delicate shades of pink and green.

Gordon Cooke (UK) uses oxides and stains in an unusual technique that enables him to produce fascinating colour textures on white porcelain. No glazes are involved and the designs remain very sharp when fired. Oxides mixed with a little powdered porcelain body are brushed on to plastic wads of clay and, inverted on to smooth plaster bats, this coloured surface is quickly dried. When rolled out, this stiffer face cracks and stretches so that the colour separates into strands which he can manipulate in various ways. The slabs are then cut and assembled into shapes and forms which are very much his own. The principles involved in this process of drying one face of a wad of clay are basically the same as used by **Len Castle** (New Zealand) for his heavily textured sculptural forms, but Gordon Cooke, working with fairly small-scale porcelain, exercises much more precise control over the surface patterns as they develop.

ABOVE: Porcelain pots, rolled and slabbed with rubbed-in oxides on 'landscape' panels. Heights 7in(17.8cm) and 8½in(21.6cm). Fired in an electric kiln to 1250°C. By GORDON COOKE (UK), 1981.

ABOVE: Porcelain vase with black, magnesium glaze fired in an electric kiln to cone 10. Height 6¹¹⁄₁₆in(17cm). By VIVIENNE FOLEY (UK), 1982.

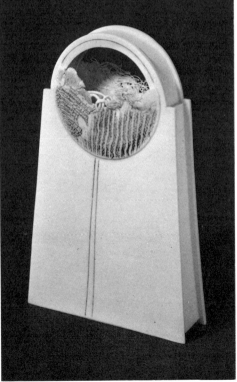

Slabbed and press-moulded porcelain with colour stains. Height 6in(15.2cm). Fired in an electric kiln to 1250°C. By GORDON COOKE (UK), 1981.

James Rothrock (USA) uses a porcelain body formulated so as to retain good plasticity after slip-casting (Grolleg 50 parts; Custer feldspar 30 parts; flint 20 parts; talc 3 parts). This allows him to manipulate and freely alter vessel forms when taken from the moulds, thus expanding the potential of the process. The bisqued pots are sanded smooth before oxides are applied with brush and pen to the soft, porous surface of the ware. The insides are glazed and the work is then fired to cone 10 to form a vitreous, translucent porcelain. The oxides are fixed into the surface during this final firing making the colours impervious to normal wear or abrasion ("the pieces are tough, don't chip easily, and are completely dishwasher safe"). A further sanding with silicon carbide paper smooths the surface to a soft, skin-like tactility. He aims to articulate the surfaces of his pieces in a manner which he considers to be analogous to music. "Colour is used to establish rhythms that develop over the surface. Overlaid patterns and lines are used to punctuate the movement, sometimes harmoniously and at other times discordantly. A visual resonance is set up to move on the calm surface of the porcelain."

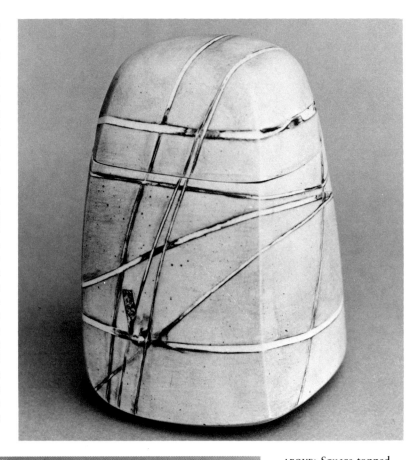

ABOVE: Square-topped covered jar, slip-cast porcelain, brushed with oxides and fired to cone 10. Height 7in(17.8cm). Exterior unglazed and polished with silicon carbide paper. By JAMES ROTHROCK (USA), 1982.

Slip-cast porcelain cups, with painted oxides and stains, unglazed but polished exterior. Height 4in(10.2cm). By JAMES ROTHROCK (USA), 1982.

Eileen Richardson (USA) makes wheel-thrown porcelain pots covered with elaborate colourful paintings (using powdered stains mixed with water, clay and a little flux) under a clear calcium glaze. Sometimes she attaches three-dimensional animals, moulded, modelled and slip-cast, near the rims of bowls and on the lids of boxes. After a low bisque firing, the design is sketched in with pencil before painting and glazing. A neutral atmosphere is maintained in the kiln to cones 10–12. The paintings are "a kind of visual memoir" incorporating all kinds of things at her home.

BELOW: 'Hibiscus'. Porcelain vase with underglaze painting. Height 7in(17.8cm). Fired to cone 10. By EILEEN RICHARDSON (USA), 1982.

ABOVE RIGHT: 'Vine'. Lidded porcelain vase. Height $14\frac{1}{2} \times 12\frac{1}{8}$in(36.2 × 30.3cm). By JOHN TAKEHARA (USA), 1982.

RIGHT: Detail of porcelain bowl, 'Black Dogs in a Black Pool', thrown and modelled, with underglaze painting. Height 7in(17.8cm), diameter 10in(25.4cm). By EILEEN RICHARDSON (USA), 1982.

ABOVE: 'Carnival ware II'. Porcelain luncheon service, colour-stained slips on bisqued ware, then covered with transparent glaze and fired to cone 7. By DOROTHY HAFNER (USA), 1982.

Stoneware dish, feldspathic base glaze with colour glazes painted and slip-trailed on top before firing in a reduction atmosphere. Diameter 8in(20.3cm). Colours obtained from chrome and copper oxides. By JANICE TCHALENKO (UK), 1982.

Janice Tchalenko produces reduction-fired stoneware which she decorates directly on top of the unfired base glaze with coloured glazes trailed and painted. Her linear patterns, grid-like or rhythmically flowing, have a spontaneous freshness. She has visited Iran where she found stimulus in richly decorated Persian ceramics.

Dorothy Hafner's influences are drawn from Japanese Oribe wares, while she also admires the richly ornamented European porcelains of the seventeenth and eighteenth centuries. Japanese textiles have also been an inspiration to her. The sub-division of her plates and dishes into a patchwork of seemingly separate patterns bears witness to these sources, but she has turned them into a highly personal idiom with designs and colours which belong firmly in the present day. Living and working in New York City she is surrounded by "geometric patterns, bright colours, blinking light and computer print-out messages" and elements of this imagery inevitably appear in her work. Porcelain provides her with the clean white ground her colours need so that, despite the inherent difficulties encountered with this material, she perseveres with its use because it has the fired strength and durability she feels essential for tableware. The forms she makes are simple in profile, reflecting her admiration of Bauhaus shapes, and thoroughly functional. The colours are applied as stained slips to the bisqued ware, which is then covered with a transparent glossy glaze fired to cone 7. Some of her designs have been handmade for, and exclusively marketed by, Tiffany and Company, and these commissions have kept her studio very busy since 1979, but she still finds time to produce individual pieces and limited editions.

So much dull tableware has filled craft shops for so long that it is refreshing to find a few imaginative studio potters who are not shy to use pattern and colour to create functional stoneware and porcelain that is full of vitality. **Janice Tchalenko** (UK) and **Dorothy Hafner** (USA) are two such potters. Their work is boldly decorated with designs which would sit equally well printed on textiles. Both are production potters, but Janice Tchalenko's work is all wheel-thrown while Dorothy Hafner's is press-moulded and slip-cast because the quantity she now produces requires reliable consistency and this is only achieved with the help of a team of four or five assistants, each with a specific responsibility for part of the making process.

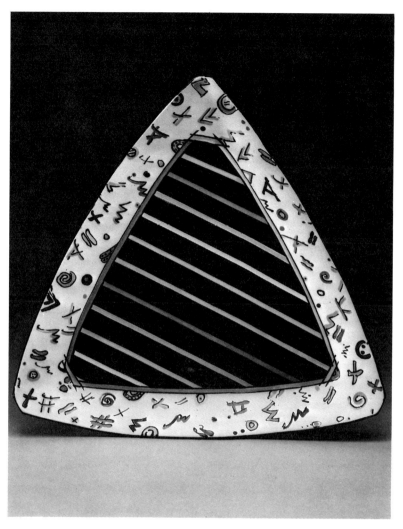

'Asterisks/Harlequin'. Porcelain platter with painted, coloured slips. 16 × 17in(40.7 × 43.2cm). By DOROTHY HAFNER (USA), 1982.

'Kyoto Homage'. Porcelain dinner service decorated with coloured slips. By DOROTHY HAFNER (USA), 1980.

6 INDIVIDUAL KILN TECHNIQUES

For many potters, the final firing carries with it an element of unpredictability. This in itself fosters excitement mixed with apprehension. The placing of the pots, the stacking arrangement of the shelves, the type of fuel, kiln atmosphere and firing pattern, the size of the kiln chamber, speed of temperature rise and fall, and even weather conditions in some cases, added to the many variables involved in the preparation and use of different materials for producing the work, are just some of the factors contributing to uncertainty.

Most of us continue searching for an unattainable ideal of one sort or another. The temptation to peep into the kiln before it is properly cooled can be overwhelming on occasions and, I must confess that, despite losing many pieces through dunting (cracking due to thermal shock) in this way, I still find it difficult to resist. I have sometimes ensured that some kind of pressing business matter or family commitment has taken me far away from my workshop so that I am prevented from fiddling with the still hot kiln on the slightest pretext.

Whether a firing has been hazardous or not, and even when the results appear to be satisfactory, the initial excitement and euphoria experienced on opening and unpacking the kiln is often replaced (for me) by a feeling of intense depression for a while. Perhaps disillusionment is caused by recognizing that nothing is as good as one had hoped or, indeed, expected it to be. I have warned my students to be prepared for this 'after-shock' and to 'sleep on it', so as to view the results of a firing afresh the following day. Later, a post-mortem is conducted on the firing itself to see how certain glazes have reacted, whether placement in the kiln has affected the behaviour of glazes and oxides, and to investigate the degree and distribution of any reduction which had

been induced. Deprived of all these risks, the life of the potter would be far less interesting and with fewer rewards. Working with clay and fire appeals to the gambling instincts in all of us. Unless we experiment with materials and processes 'to see what happens' we may not be able to make full use of the ceramic medium's potential for expressing personal ideas.

Raku bowl. Diameter 12in(30.5cm) approx. The blackened areas have resisted the white glaze by the use of masking tape. By MARTIN SMITH (UK).

OPPOSITE: 'Pedestal Piece'. Wheel-thrown and altered, low-fired in a salt bisque to about Orton cone 010 (no slips, stains or glaze). Height 14in (35.1cm), width 9in(22.9cm), depth 13in(33cm). By PAUL SOLDNER (USA), 1982.

Electric kiln firing is, normally, lacking in drama. Once a firing pattern has been established for firing familiar combinations of materials, any uncertainty concerning results is more likely to depend on glaze thicknesses and the density of any applied colour. For those who work with porcelain a further factor will be their skill in gauging variations in wall thickness, because any serious misjudgement will cause pieces to warp or collapse.

It is primarily the reduction firing process that produces the surprises. Although it is possible to create a reducing atmosphere in electric kilns (and some are specifically constructed to cater for this), very few potters will risk damaging costly wire elements by so doing. A 'reducing' or 'reduction' atmosphere occurs when the oxygen supply within the chamber is restricted. This is generally induced during firing in any of several ways according to the kiln design, fuel, or type of burners. Basically, a smoky atmosphere is generated by the presence of excess, or 'free', carbon (from the oil, gas, wood, coke or other combustibles being burnt) that is hungry for oxygen. Combustion continues with the necessary oxygen being drawn from the oxides present in the clay and glazes to unite with the carbon in the formation of carbon dioxide gas. Iron and copper oxides undergo the greatest colour transformation, the former being the normal ingredient in true celadon glazes and the latter essential for the intriguing production of copper-reds. In reduction glazes, iron can give colours ranging from delicate greens, blues and greys through deep olive to rust-red and black according to the proportions used. The usual greens and blues produced from copper oxides in glazes fired under clean, oxidizing conditions are transformed into an amazing variety of pinks, reds and purples in the reduction kiln.

Some potters spend a great deal of time and effort in search of the more elusive versions of these rich colours. Copper-reds can also be obtained quite safely, without risk to the elements in an electric kiln, by mixing a proportion of fine grade silicon carbide (usually in equal amounts to the copper oxide up to about 0.5%) in slips or glazes, thus causing a limited local reduction to take place. Tin oxide will help to stabilize the colour, and approximately 1% added to the glaze will be sufficient in most recipes to prevent the copper re-oxidizing on cooling.

Reducing conditions are also necessary

Three wheel-thrown pots, raw-glazed with feldspathic mixtures containing various colourants (a) porcelain bowl with titanium-copper, 1980 (b) tall porcelain vase with zinc-barium-nickel-titanium, 1981 (c) stoneware jar with chrome-nickel-titanium, 1979. Tallest piece $16\frac{1}{8}$in(41cm). Reduction fired in a gas kiln to 1380°C with salt added. By HEINER BALZAR (West Germany).

for the formation of lustres. In the case of commercially prepared on-glaze lustres, the metallic salts are locally reduced by the burning off of the resinous medium in which they are carried. A reduction 'atmosphere' on the other hand, is induced by re-lighting burners and adjusting the ratio of air to fuel input at particular temperatures (between 600° and 700°C) in flame kilns during the cooling period, to obtain certain metallic lustres.

The tremendous enthusiasm for raku over the last twenty years or so has encouraged a great deal of direct inventive experiment with different forms of post-firing reduction processes. **Paul Soldner** (USA) is perhaps the leading exponent of raku and it was certainly due to his initial, adventurous approach in handling materials and developing techniques that the processes involved in raku became so popular in the West. The more esoteric spirituality underlying traditional Japanese raku has been largely ignored by many of those who have explored firing methods merely as a means to obtaining certain surface qualities. The word 'raku' itself relates to what might be called a concept of contemplative happiness, but its mystical and philosophical associations with Zen Buddhism have been of only incidental interest to most Western potters. Paul Soldner, writing in *Ceramic Review* (No. 22, July/August 1973) said that: "with the exception of the term 'serendipity', I know of no other single English word as suitable as 'raku'" for describing this kind of pottery "made within a framework of mental expectation". He suggests that raku is an attitude rather than a process, placing the emphasis upon "the beauty of the accidental and spontaneous, asymmetry, value of, and appreciation for, nature undominated or controlled by man".

The unique qualities obtainable through the process of raku ceramics as a means of personal expression have, nevertheless, provided the greatest stimulus for the majority of those potters who have concentrated their efforts in this field.

Basically, the technique involves the use of low-fired glazes on an open-textured clay body resistant to thermal shock. Pieces are usually placed in the kiln chamber at temperatures in excess of 750°C. The potter, protected by heavy gauntlets, uses long-handled metal tongs for this purpose. The pots are removed by the same means when the glaze has melted. They are then subjected to further treatment, the simplest of

Vessel form, wheel-thrown and altered, black/white with iron and copper calligraphy, post-firing reduction. Height 20in(50.8cm), width 11in(28cm). By PAUL SOLDNER (USA), 1980.

which is immersion in a bucket of water. This causes most glazes to craze and produce characteristic crackle patterns. Pieces are often covered with sawdust, wet leaves, grasses, seaweed, or similar organic substances, immediately on being taken from the kiln. Dense smoke is formed, permeating the body and colouring it from grey to black according to the length of time it remains in this state of post-firing reduction. White glazes develop strong, black crackle lines while glazes containing copper and iron oxides may give a variety of colours and lustrous effects (sometimes from just one glaze) on the surface of a single piece.

Recent work by Paul Soldner, however, is not subjected to the post-firing reduction period generally associated with raku. Instead, his pieces are packed around with a selection of combustible materials in the kiln and fired to 1100°C or less. The addition of a little salt produces coloured flashings on the pots depending upon the degree of reduction, the amount of salt, and the oxide content of slips used to coat areas of the form.

Most clays can be adapted for raku work if between 25% and 50% grog is first mixed into the body. A preliminary firing to 1000°–1100°C (according to the type of clay) is normally undertaken, followed by low-temperature glazing and firing in the range 750°–850°C.

Although it was the English potter, **Bernard Leach**, who first brought raku to the notice of studio potters in the West, it was the less inhibited Americans who took it up seriously and developed it as a means of expressive art. **Walter Dexter** (Canada) was stimulated by what he calls "the vitality of the Americans" and their "try it and see" approach to ceramics. He also acknowledges influences from Japanese folk pottery, but his colourful raku pots are very much his own personal response to the medium. Some of his pieces are made from several sections. Sharp changes of direction in profile (for example, at the shoulder) of some of his forms result from inverting thrown pots. Necks are then added to what would other-

ABOVE RIGHT: 'Wall-piece'. Bas-relief raku, concave impressed slab, grey/black/white colours (unglazed) from post-firing reduction (smoke). 20 × 18in(50.8 × 45.7cm). By PAUL SOLDNER (USA), 1978.

RIGHT: Long-necked raku vase thrown in sections and joined with blue and yellow pigments on white crackle glaze (black areas unglazed). Height 15in(38.1cm) approx. By WALTER DEXTER (Canada), 1980.

wise have been the base. He decorates the surfaces with engobes (slips) of very fine-grained clays mixed with glaze, which fuse together well. Hay is often used, rather than sawdust, to obtain a 'gentler' post-firing reduction effect after the pot it taken red-hot from the kiln. This more immediate involvement at such close quarters with flame and smoke has brought him a greater freedom than he had previously enjoyed when working in stoneware. It has loosened up his attitude and approach to all ceramics.

Some potters will subject raku pots to re-firing and further reduction several times, perhaps adding extra coats of oxides, nit-rates, or chlorides to achieve lustred, colour-stained and smoked areas on the surface.

Joan Campbell (Australia) fires her 'ho-rizon' forms in a large trolley kiln. She spends a long time 'setting' the pieces for the kiln so that the seaweed she uses will mark

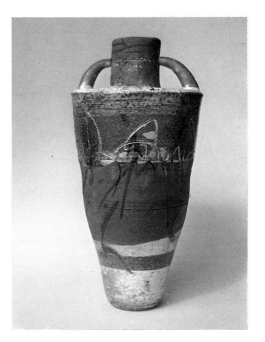

Wheel-thrown raku vase (thrown in two sections) part white-glazed, brushed copper oxide (reduced to red) at upper part of body. Height 15in(38.1cm) approx. By WALTER DEXTER (Canada), 1979.

BELOW: 'Horizons'. Raku form, hand-built, slip and seaweed smoked decoration. 36 × 36in (91.4 × 91.4cm). By JOAN CAMPBELL (Australia), 1981.

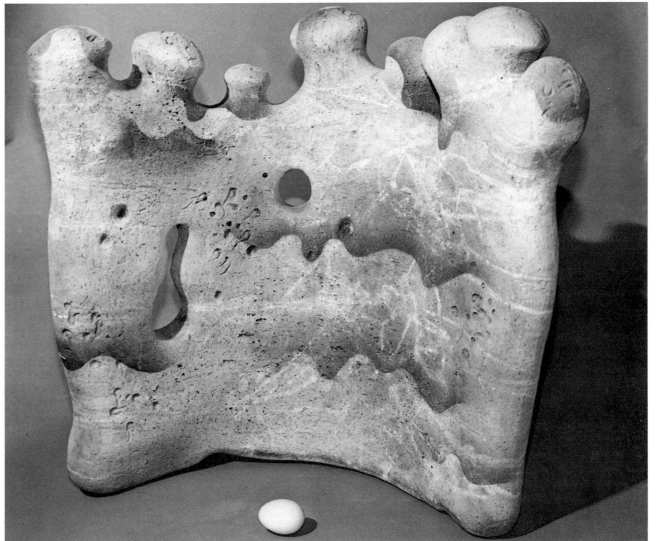

them in particular ways. The kiln is fired up to 900°–950°C before it is opened ("it's quite a blast!") and, with the help of an assistant, she lifts pieces out and on to a waiting platform. Then ("with a quick breath") they are lifted again and swung into a prepared smoke pit. It is difficult to obtain a harmonious smoke pattern which is complementary to the slip and seaweed decoration on these unusually shaped pieces so, after removal from the smoke, she uses a gas torch to burn away any areas of smoke stain that appear too heavy. This treatment may take between five and seven minutes, in order to draw out the colour values that she senses are needed for full realization of the form. "It's always intuitive. Pot and potter really have to work as one and, perhaps, it is this intimacy with clay and fire that keeps the work so vitally interesting. The unexpected beauty revealed through the combination of natural forces keeps me forever aware of my ignorance, and lightens my heavy-handed efforts." She is excited to be working increasingly within the earthenware range of temperatures.

The traditions of raku are certainly of far less interest to **Jeff Mincham** (Australia) than the actual process. He has gradually adapted more or less simple functional vessel forms as vehicles for his own personal imagery. He has learnt to control surface effects within a fair degree of predictability. Recently he has been moving away from deliberately decorating and drawing on to the surface of pots. Now he is pursuing "the feeling of moving shadows, tones and colours across the surface" which comes closer to capturing the essence of landscapes that inspire him. The utility of such pots is often of little relevance to him and he finds it easier "to think as a painter might, rather than as a potter". Some of his pots are quite large and he has built a special 'lift-off' or 'top-hat' type of kiln with ceramic fibre insulation to simplify the firing and handling of these.

Monique Ferron (Canada) was attracted to raku because of its "directness and simplicity". Following research into its origins, she became sympathetic towards Zen philosophy and concerned for certain qualities in ceramic art. Despite being influenced by Oriental art, it has been "a sort of adventure in the imaginary world" and a more abstract form of expression that has emerged in her work. This appears to her to be more reflective of contemporary civilization. For post-firing reduction she simply places the glowing pieces direct from the kiln (cones

ABOVE: Large lidded raku jar, wheel-thrown, brushed white slip and sprayed clear glaze. Height 16½in(42cm). Fired to 1060°C followed by reduction process. By JEFF MINCHAM (Australia), 1982.

'Sphere'. Coiled raku pot, cone 08 glazes with post-firing reduction. Diameter 18in(45.7cm). By MONIQUE FERRON (Canada), 1979.

RIGHT: Large raku jar, clear crackle glaze over white slip, sprayed copper oxide top and bottom. Fired to 1060°C. Height 23in(58.4cm) approx. By JEFF MINCHAM (Australia), 1982.

08–07) on to layers of organic matter such as leaves, hay, paper and so on, and immediately covers them with a metal container appropriate to their size and shape. This is kept as airtight as possible until cool enough to handle. However, air does occasionally 'leak' into the container and this affects the oxides in an unpredictable way.

All the work of **Karin Hessenberg** (UK) is made from a porcelain body thrown and turned on the wheel. Most of her pots are altered from the round to an elliptical section. They are often cut, overlapped and rejoined to make the simple bowl forms lean or twist. When leather-hard some of these pots are burnished and then later bisque fired to 950°–980°C in an electric kiln. This strengthens them and preserves the burnish before sawdust firing in a shallow kiln.

Her method of sawdust firing is very fast. Most firings are completed in two or three hours. The pots are placed on a bed of sawdust and wood shavings in a small dry-bricked kiln of about 3 ft sq. floor area, with walls about 18 in. to 2 ft high. More wood shavings and sawdust are piled thinly on the pots; two or three layers being built up in this way. A vigorous fire is lit on top to catch the whole area of sawdust alight. The fast

firing creates the blotchy, speckled effect she wants. To make striped, spotted or straw patterns on the pots she has adapted a technique used by the Bizen potters of Japan, who protected areas of their pots with pads of refractory clay. This prevents random glazing from flying wood ash in the kiln. Karin Hessenberg uses freshly rolled-out pads of plastic clay to prevent blackening parts of the surface. Pieces of paper or straw are placed between the pads and the pot. This material smoulders and 'imprints' marks on the surface.

'Vaisseaux' (Vessels) triptych. Raku, hand-built, glazes sprayed. Height of tallest triptych $20\frac{7}{8}$in(53cm). Fired to cone 08. By MONIQUE FERRON (Canada), 1980.

'Twist Bowl with Diamond Spots'. Porcelain body bisqued to 980°C before smoking in a sawdust firing. Height 5in(12.2cm). The piece is wheel-thrown, turned, cut and rejoined while leather-hard. By KARIN HESSENBERG (UK), 1982.

Another potter working with burnished porcelain is **Debbie Pointon** (New Zealand). Her silver-inlaid pots are pre-bisqued to 1000°C and then smoked in a metal drum packed with wood chips and seaweed. She then takes a 'rubbing' of the design she has carved at the leather-hard stage. The rubbing is made on a self-adhesive paper label which is transferred to a sheet of sterling silver and the shape cut out with a piercing saw. Several hours of careful filing are required to ensure that the silver fits perfectly. Finally, the metal is polished and glued into position.

Other smoked pots made by Debbie Pointon are flashed with black, white and orange markings obtained by packing the pots in charcoal-filled saggars placed in a ceramic fibre kiln fired with liquid petroleum gas to 1230°C. The flames dance around the pieces leaving smoke marks on the unglazed surfaces.

'Flame Spirit'. Teapot, fumed porcelain, thrown and modelled, fired in saggar packed with charcoal to 1230°C. By DEBBIE POINTON (New Zealand), 1982.

Smoked porcelain bowl with sterling silver inlay. Height $6\frac{5}{16}$in(16cm). Wheel-thrown, turned and incised, bisqued to 1000°C, followed by smoking with wood chips and seaweed prior to inlaying silver. By DEBBIE POINTON (New Zealand), 1982.

Charcoal is also used by **Philip Cornelius** (USA) but in a once-fired process. Unglazed greenware, without any oxide or slipped decoration, is stacked in the kiln, no supporting shelves being used. Pots are placed on top of each other with wads of refractory clay separating them. Firing proceeds with natural gas fuel until 1260°–1300°C. Charcoal is then introduced on top of the ware by a chute made from a length of angle-iron. The resulting surface is similar in parts to a salt firing, but with much broader effects in blacks, blues, greys and reds depending on the nature of the charcoal covering and the direction of the draught. When very thin porcelain is fired in this way the charcoal is first ground into finer particles so that it will not break the ware as it falls.

Similar variegated colour flashings can be obtained by packing pots (especially porcelain or whitewares) in saggars with alternating layers of sawdust and sand. Oxides, such as copper and iron, together with salt, can be mixed with this and other combustible matter in small amounts for different colours and surface qualities. Sand alone will resist the effects of smoke. Patterns can be controlled to some degree by the angle at which a pot is packed into the saggar. **Sebastian Blackie** (UK) fires many of his pieces to 1250°C under constant reduction from 800°C in sawdust-filled brick saggars. No glazes are used except that which is naturally formed from ash deposits, while some areas are resisted by sand. The kiln is crash-cooled to 900°C over a one-hour period. The clay body he uses is specially formulated with a high feldspar content designed to accentuate flashing, and with varying quantities of red clay and china clay to exploit the colour range. He sometimes deliberately fires his kiln unevenly with as much as a 300°C difference across one piece of work. This may result in the clay beginning to melt in one part while remaining soft and porous in another. He finds that crash-cooling is essential to avoid dunting and to maximise firing marks. Sebastian Blackie is excited by the plasticity of clay and by the drama of fire, and feels that the art of ceramics has broadened beyond accepted

ABOVE RIGHT: 'Indian Hill'. Teapot, charcoal-fired porcelain. Height 8in(23cm). By PHILIP CORNELIUS (USA), 1981.

RIGHT: Bowl, stoneware, coiled, scraped and cut. Fired to 1250°C (under continuous reduction from 800°C). Width 19in(48.3cm), depth 5in(12.7cm). By SEBASTIAN BLACKIE (UK), 1981.

forms of functionalism to reflect "the somewhat schizophrenic nature of our society".

All manner of random surface colours can
be produced through the use of light-
coloured clays (or darker bodies coated with
white slip) in this kind of saggar firing.
Results will vary according to the nature of
the additional material placed in the saggar,
and the effects will be further conditioned if
a piece has been coated with glaze. Again,
the oxides of copper are particularly useful.
Small pottery containers filled with copper
oxide placed in close proximity to a piece in
the kiln will cause grey, pink, or red blushes
to appear on the surface, albeit in an
unpredictable way. If iron and copper
oxides are sprayed on to unglazed porcelain
prior to placing a pot into a saggar containing some dry salt, pale pinks through to deep
rust-reds can be produced. Such saggars
would need to be sealed to prevent volatile
materials from affecting any other pieces in
the same kiln.

Thrown form (three
sections, assembled),
stoneware, fired to
1250°C (with continuous
reduction from 800°C).
Height 21in(53.3cm). By
SEBASTIAN BLACKIE (UK),
1981.

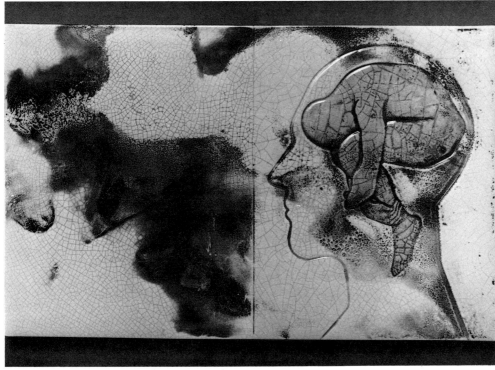

BELOW: 'I know'. Slip-
cast ceramic with several
firings of glaze up to
1040°C. 16 × 10in
(40.6 × 25.4cm). Crackle
stained with inks and
pink underglaze colour.
Finally smoked. By
GLENYS BARTON (UK),
1981.

ABOVE: Stoneware wine bottle with cane handle and stopper. Height 13⅜in(34cm). Fired with liquid petroleum gas to 1300°C. By MIREK SMIŠEK (New Zealand), 1982.

More conventional salt glazing has enjoyed considerable popularity among studio potters during the past twenty years or so. In Britain, much of the initial stimulus came from potters who took the vocational course originally set up at Harrow School of Art by **Victor Margrie** and **Michael Casson**. Many ex-Harrow students have continued in this tradition to develop their own personal styles. Salt glaze in the twentieth century had been relegated to the coating of industrial ceramics, such as sewer and drainage pipes, until potters around the world began to explore its potential afresh. The characteristic 'orange peel' texture of this type of glaze is well-suited to both relief and incised designs, since the glaze does not obscure details. The traditional greys and browns of this glaze come from the iron content of the

Large lidded jar, salt-glazed stoneware, thrown. Height 17½in(44.5cm). Spiral produced with a throwing rib on the wet pot from bottom to top as it revolves; sprayed with cobalt and manganese mixture. Fired to 1280°C. By WALTER KEELER (UK), 1982.

Stoneware teapot, salt glaze over iron-bearing slip, 1300°C in reduction. By JANET MANSFIELD (Australia), 1981.

BELOW RIGHT: Salt-glazed stoneware jug, thrown, with cut rim and extruded handle. Height 11½in(29.2cm). Fired to 1280°C. By WALTER KEELER (UK), 1982.

clay. Coloured glazes or slips are often trailed, painted, dipped, sprayed or resisted on the ware before firing with salt. Very rich colourings with great depth can result.

Glazing with salt offers certain economies because most potters fire their work only once without the cost of a pre-bisque. However, salt is very corrosive, attacking the kiln lining and furniture quite relentlessly. Therefore, some of the financial advantages are offset against the cost of replacements. Salt combines with the silica content of clay to form sodium silicate and this chemical action also gradually eats away the brick fabric of the kiln. In order to protect kiln shelves and props from salt glaze the tops and sides are usually coated with a wash of alumina and china clay.

Stoneware vase with two glazes superimposed. Height 7½in(19cm). Wood-fired to 1300°C in reduction. Salt was thrown into the kiln at the end of the firing before clamming up. By CLAUDE CHAMPY (France), 1982.

RIGHT: Earthenware pot with lid. Height 8¼in(21cm). This pot is made from a white clay, thrown, turned and then polished with the back of a rubber kidney. Raw slipped with a levigated red slip, the surface quality depends entirely on the firing. (The pot was waxed after leaving the kiln.) Wood-fired in reduction to 1050°C. By PIERRE BAYLE (France), 1982.

ABOVE: Thrown and squared vases with trailed glaze decoration. Salt-glazed stoneware. Fired to 1285°C. By JANE HAMLYN (UK), 1982.

Lidded jar, thrown, salt-glazed stoneware with trailed glaze decoration. Fired to 1285°C. By JANE HAMLYN (UK), 1982.

Salt-glaze kilns used for a once-fired process are heated slowly at first, as for any bisque firing. Reduction may be commenced around 1000°C. Wet salt is introduced through special ports towards the latter stages of the firing. **Jane Hamlyn** (UK) begins salting her kiln at 1235°C following a period of up to an hour during which an oxidising atmosphere is maintained to assist the removal of any carbon remaining in the body. She throws between $\frac{1}{2}$ to 1 lb of salt into the kiln every ten minutes through two ports in the front wall of her kiln. About 28 lbs of salt are used in her 60 cu. ft kiln in this one-and-a-half-hour salting and soaking period, until the pyrometric cone bends around 1285°C. Placement in the kiln will determine the degree of exposure to salt vapours and pots will be affected accordingly.

The advent of ceramic fibre insulation material in various forms (blanket, board, block, and so on), first developed for the heat-resistant surfaces essential to the space industry, are being increasingly used in kiln construction. This material has proved to be extremely efficient, giving economical firings in terms of both time and cost. It has also led to some revolutionary firing techniques. **Alan Peascod** (Australia), in company with other potters I met in Australia, has been able to ignore those established rules binding potters using conventional fire-brick kilns. Ceramic fibre allows much faster firing and cooling to be conducted without risk to the pots. The material does not soak up and radiate heat as does firebrick insulation. Alan Peascod has, on occasions, fired the same piece three times to stoneware temperatures in the one kiln lined with ceramic fibre. This immediacy and speed of handling permits re-glazing and overlaying of colours while the idea is still fresh. In other kilns one single glost firing to 1280°C can average out at thirty hours or more before results can be examined.

For ten years **Karen Karnes** (USA) worked with salt glaze but changed to wood firing when she moved to Vermont. She now uses a 100 cu. ft kiln and the greater placing space has led ("unconsciously at first") to an increase in the size of her pots. Her primary interest has always been in form, but she wants the firing to add a "coloured skin" to the ware. Previously, salt glazing added richness to the surface of brushed slips, but her present kiln fires so efficiently that very little flying ash is deposited on the pots and she has to use a 'dry' glaze to bring out the colour. Variable glaze thicknesses are now an important element in her work.

Wayne Ngan (Canada) uses an 85 cu. ft kiln fired with wood and oil. In some of his firing experiments he burns "dry driftwoods from the seashore, dry seaweed, hazelnut shells, salt pork, old sweaters, ashes from stoves and fireplaces, and so on". His clay body and glazes are made up from local materials and include an 'oil spot' black glaze made from a local earthenware clay. He finds it exciting to use materials from his own environment.

New kiln technology includes the invention of extremely accurate digital read-out pyrometers able to sense and indicate the slightest fluctuations in temperature. A particularly interesting instrument, proving valuable to studio potters, was developed by the Commonwealth Scientific and Industrial Research Organization (CSIRO) in Australia. Called an Oxygen Probe, it consists of a high alumina sheath fitted with an oxygen-sensitive pellet of zirconia-yttria at one end and a terminal box at the other. Inside the sheath a second tube is fitted with a platinum/platinum 13% rhodium thermocouple. The tip of this thermocouple is held in contact with the inside face of the oxygen-sensitive pellet, and the outer surface of the pellet is connected to a platinum wire leading back to the terminal box. A sample of fresh air is continuously fed to the probe by means of an air hose and a tiny pump. Differences in oxygen content between the fresh air and the kiln atmosphere cause a voltage to be generated by the zirconia pellet and this is registered by the digital meter. Atmospheric and temperature readings are individually given thus enabling much more sensitive control and, of course, greater efficiency in firing than any other method I know.

ABOVE LEFT: Salt-glazed vase with cut sides and dark slip (cobalt/copper/iron), fired with wood and oil. Height 13in(33cm). By WAYNE NGAN (Canada), 1981.

ABOVE RIGHT: Covered jar with distinctive wire-cut lid. Wood fired. Height 19in(48.3cm). By KAREN KARNES (USA), 1982.

RIGHT: 'Wolley Zuff'. Thrown and altered earthenware, multi-fired with various glazes maturing between cones 06 and 09. 15 × 14 × 13in (38.1 × 35.6 × 33cm). All this artist's current work is especially concerned with colour, complementing surface and form. By HARVEY GOLDMAN (USA), 1982. Courtesy of Impressions Gallery, Boston.

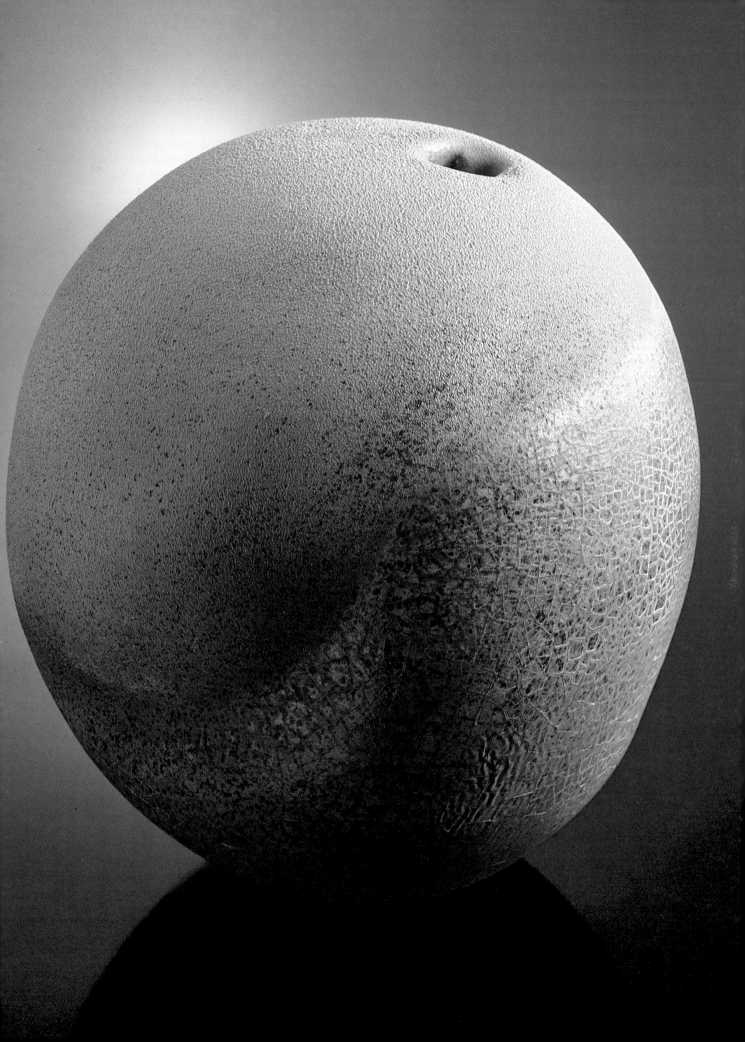

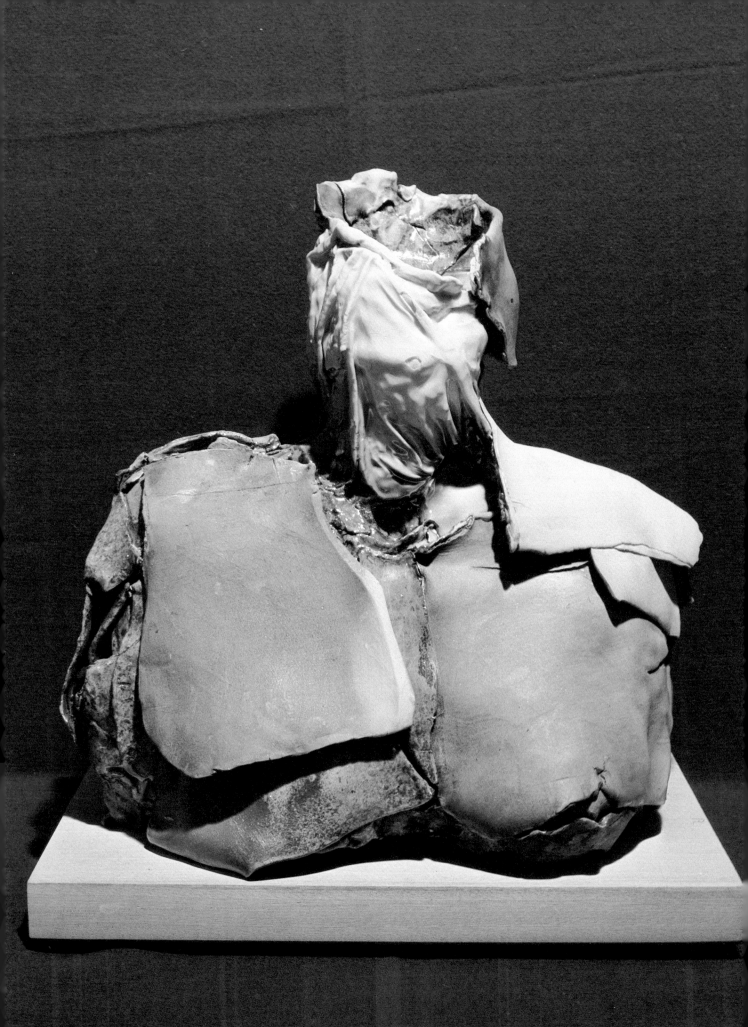

7 FUTURE PROSPECTS

Future developments in studio ceramics can only be a matter for conjecture. The current situation, approaching the mid-1980s, appears to be reasonably healthy, despite the ever-present economic problems which have caused several long-established galleries and craft shops to cease trading.

OPPOSITE: 'Bust'. Hand-built porcelain with lustres. Fired to 1400°C. By MARIA KUCZYNSKA (Poland), 1982.

Mixed media sculpture, composed of slip-cast ceramic 'rocks' (low-fired and coloured with oxides and watercolours) with sand, paper and wood. 8 × 3 × 3ft (2.5 × 0.9 × 0.9m). This piece was completed by the artist while teaching at the University of Tasmania, Australia. By GUDRUN KLIX (USA), 1982.

Teapot, stoneware with
trailed and painted
coloured glazes on
white. Reduction fired.
By JANICE TCHALENKO
(UK), 1982.

Various factors must be taken into ac-
count in attempting to assess prospects for
continued growth. The first of these, concerning the basic human need for fulfilment
and worthwhile experience, responsible for
bringing so many people into the crafts, has
already been mentioned. Some potters may
never become known outside a small circle
of friends and relations, yet they achieve
sufficient satisfaction through working with
clay to sustain their interest.

A vast industry has grown up to supply
the equipment and materials required for
ceramics. This industry has become so competitive that sophisticated machinery and
refined materials are now widely available at
reasonable prices. The latest technology is
no guarantee of better ceramics, but it does
mean that considerable business interests

back the craft potter today where there were
very few only a relatively short time ago.

Local, regional, national and even international organizations are now firmly in
existence, giving a corporate strength which
should not be underestimated. Exhibitions,
films, books and magazines devoted to
studio ceramics proliferate. Sponsorship of
one kind or another has ensured that some
potters have become household names and a
few even legends in their own lifetimes. Lest
potters become complacent and too comfort-
tably secure in the present situation, however, there is one overriding element that
cannot be ignored: the consumer.

A shift towards more colourful decorated
ceramics has emerged during the 1970s and
80s, but this has been part of the natural
process of change rather than a response to

Teapot, wheel-thrown and pushed back while wet, extruded handle. Height 7⅞in(20cm). Blue grey slip under a salt glaze, fired to 1280°C. By WALTER KEELER (UK), 1982.

consumer demand. The best potters, in any case, create their own markets through the originality and consistent quality of their work. A complex and variable network of influences, never static, favours certain developments at the expense of others for a time, only to swing round again as new trends appear.

Fashions come and go in all things. Human nature demands variety and change but on terms that are difficult to predict. Good taste and even standards continue to be subjects for much debate. Both are virtually impossible to define to the satisfaction of everyone, unless kept within certain parameters. Fickleness and caprice are no strangers to art.

Studio ceramics today are not essential consumer products like food, shelter, warmth or clothing. With a few exceptions, the finest industrially made tablewares cannot be equalled for price, and the choice offered is extremely wide (including a number of 'studio lines' from major manufacturers that imitate craft pottery). And yet the best handmade ceramics possess intrinsic qualities that no machine yet devised can successfully produce. The uniqueness of such pieces and the human contact communicated through the work are special ingredients evoking empathy.

The percentage of the British population purchasing the work of studio potters is fairly small. One might hazard a guess that output is beginning to exceed demand especially where the usual jugs and ubiquitous mugs are concerned.

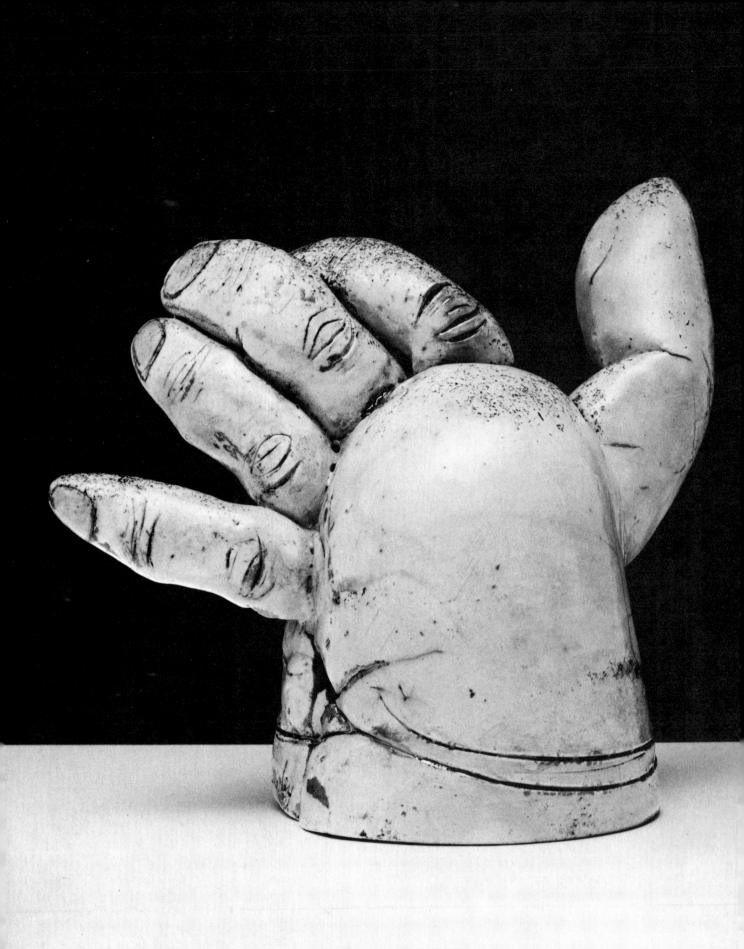

Relief panel, white stoneware, press-moulded 'stones' with rubbed oxides, once fired to 1280°C in an electric kiln. Mounted on aluminium plate 3ft 3⅜in(1m) square approx. By ULLA VIOTTI (Sweden), 1980.

Herein lies a dilemma. Should the studio potter, whether making utilitarian or non-functional ceramics, attempt to gauge the market and produce pieces which he thinks will easily sell, or should he satisfy his own creative instincts irrespective of cost? The market itself consists of several identifiable layers from knick-knackish clutter to the more esoteric art objects. Most potters who support themselves entirely out of the proceeds from sales of their work make a 'bread and butter' line of pots that they are confident will sell. Some admit to this in an almost apologetic way as if they have pros-tituted their art. Others enjoy the rhythm and discipline imposed by repetition work to such an extent that any diversion into one-off pieces is rarely felt to be necessary. Many leading potters also teach, either as their primary occupation or by freelancing around the colleges. Those who do so are often less affected by the whims of the market-place. They are unlikely to play safe at the expense of personal satisfaction and, if their work is good enough, are more able to make sufficient impact to become popular and 'collectible'.

When Bernard Leach set up his studio and workshop at St Ives in 1920 he was probably the only potter in the whole of Cornwall. Today, few villages in that county do not boast a potter in residence. In my own county of Norfolk, where I came to live and work in 1966, the number of potters has multiplied at all levels and it appears to be true of many others parts of Britain. This large-scale migration of potters to the rural areas and smaller country towns has been due to the cheaper price of properties with workshop space, reduced overheads, and also the attractions of a slower, more tranquil pace of life. It seems doubtful that this rapid growth, on a sound commercial basis, can be maintained.

OPPOSITE: 'Hand'. Raku, hand-built. Height 10⅝in(27cm). By JILL CROWLEY (UK), 1982.

Fortunately, more people are seriously collecting individual pieces of studio ceramics now, albeit generally at the top end of the market. Some may do so with an eye to future values and sale-room prospects, but most collectors of my own acquaintance are knowledgeable and enthusiastic about their collections. Above all, they buy for their own pleasure. Some collect only the work of established potters; some confine their interest to a selected few, whose careers they follow closely; others tour the annual degree shows in search of new talent.

Any would-be collector is advised to visit some of the galleries and museums listed in the appendices of this book in order to familiarise him/herself with the range of available work. In this way personal preferences will emerge and the styles of particular craftsmen will become recognizable. Many gallery owners are quite well acquainted with the philosophies and working methods of the potters whose work they sell, and they are usually pleased to talk about individual pieces to prospective, interested customers.

Other useful sources of information are the guides and handbooks published by crafts societies and potters' guilds. These often give details about potters whose workshops may be visited, or places where their work may be seen and purchased. In Britain, the Craftsmen Potters' Association publishes *Potters* which is a regularly updated directory of the work of over 150 full members. Also the Crafts Council produces a similar guide entitled *Craftsmen of Quality* listing potters and other craftsmen whose work is included in a selective index composed of colour slides, photographs and personal information. In addition, ceramics magazines (see Bibliography on page 248) constantly reflect current trends or innovations and offer informative articles on all asepcts of the subject, and most public libraries stock a good selection of books dealing with the history, appreciation and technicalities of ceramics. References abound for anyone who wishes to research the field both before and during collecting contemporary work.

A surprising and unfortunate number of ceramics graduates, who produce promising work for their finals exhibitions, seem to disappear without trace soon after leaving the stimulating and somewhat protected environment of their colleges. Their inspiration seems to wither away, like a delicate plant removed from the security of the

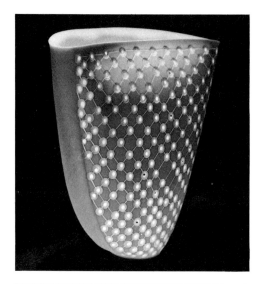

Bone china form, slip-cast, incised and pierced surface, polished. Height $4\frac{5}{16}$in(11cm). By ANGELA VERDON (UK), 1982.

Porcelain pot, thrown and turned, cream and orange-brown shiny and matt glazes. Height $3\frac{1}{2}$in(8.9cm). Fired to 1280°C in an electric kiln. By GEOFFREY SWINDELL (UK), 1980.

hothouse, unless they have the determination to persevere in their work. Loans and grants are available to assist new craftsmen to set up workshops and such schemes have, undoubtedly, sustained many who might otherwise have succumbed to inertia in the face of daunting financial obstacles.

Sadly, in times of severe stringency only very few can benefit in this way. Education should be the inalienable right of all who seek it, yet it is often the first area to suffer when governmental policies demand cuts in public spending. In fact, the reverse should be the case to ensure that opportunities for rewarding and meaningful activities are increased rather than diminished. Ultimately, more people may then be encouraged to learn how to make things for nothing but the sheer enjoyment of doing so.

Craft shops and privately owned commercial galleries also have an important role which tends to be overlooked or under-

'Aerial View'. Porcelain
box with incised and
painted design.
12 × 14 × 7in
(30.5 × 35.6 × 17.8cm). By
PAULA WINOKUR (USA),
1981.

valued. They provide the craftsmen with
much more than just a useful sales outlet.
The better gallery owners get to know the
potters well enough to promote their interests and, by displaying pieces to the best
advantage, they are able to inform and
educate the public about the work. Few such
galleries are subsidized from any public
funds. Instead, they have to back their own
judgement as to their stock or the mounting
of specialist exhibitions. In so doing they
supply a service without which the crafts
would not have gained such prominence and
respectability. Good pieces of work need
plenty of space around them if they are to be
appreciated. Properly displayed and well-lit
objects are far more likely to attract a
purchaser than if they are crowded together
with others or placed against unsympathetic
backgrounds. The galleries, therefore, have
the facilities and the expertise which, if
sensitively handled, can benefit both crafts-

men and public in equal measure.

Compared to painting and sculpture,
most studio ceramics are still reasonably
priced for any would-be collectors. The
request for pieces by particular potters may
be greater than the supply and, inevitably,
their prices will be higher. Anyone fortunate
enough to have purchased a good piece by
someone like **Hans Coper**, for example, ten
years ago, will not only have enjoyed
owning it but will also be aware that its
monetary value has escalated enormously in
a short time. This is a feature of twentieth-
century studio ceramics which, now established, seems certain to continue.

Earlier in this chapter I referred to an
increasing interest in more colourful, decorated ceramics among both potters and
their public. This in turn has prompted a
revival in the use of earthenwares and low-
firing techniques. White burning bodies,
including porcelain, which allow pure col-

ABOVE: 'Vertical Structure'. Slip-cast terracotta panel. Height 29½in(75cm). By NINO CARUSO (Italy), 1978.

ours to be achieved unsullied by iron stain, are enjoying considerable popularity as we approach the mid-1980s. Chance effects realized through the almost random action of a reduction firing upon iron-bearing bodies no longer hold the dominant position in the galleries that they did a few years ago. More and more potters are now decorating their pieces with precise patterns in brushwork, resists or direct carving and in this way retain greater control of the final result. Oxidized firing and the use of electric kilns, often accepted as more suitable for working in an urban environment than flame kilns, need not be considered a poor substitute for, or in any way inferior to, working with reduction atmospheres.

The emotional and physical involvement, the excitement, the delights and despairs, the highs and lows are probably greater with flame kilns but there remains also a stronger element of unpredictability which many potters feel able to reject. Those 'natural' qualities of materials, so revered by adherents to the one-time inviolate 'Leach tradition', are not of such paramount importance. Indeed, some potters even spurn the use of glaze and prefer to paint their ceramic with emulsion or acrylic colours to ensure absolute control over the final product.

The wheel of fashion is never still. As it

'Now'. Unglazed bone china elements individually made and assembled on wooden support. Height 5ft 3in(1.6m). By ANNA ZAMORSKA (Poland), 1981, wood by R. ZAMORSKI.

'Teapot'. Slab-built, black-stained porcelain, inlaid with coloured elements, fired to 1240°C. Height 8in(20.3cm). By DOROTHY FEIBLEMAN (UK), 1982.

turns, techniques and processes are resurrected, revised or invented only to be discarded when ideas develop, moods or feelings alter, and tastes change. One can often detect trends as they begin to emerge, although the future may still remain uncertain. Undoubtedly, ideas or objects which seem novel or unusual are more likely to catch the attention whatever the response they evoke. But in time they become familiar, invite less comment and eventually are replaced by something else. Twenty or thirty years later they may be rediscovered, redeveloped, explored afresh and given new life.

It is easy to condemn change and to confine acceptance to that which is well-tried or familiar. It requires a degree of courage to express radical ideas against the mainstream of established practice, especially in an ancient craft like ceramics. But it must surely be wiser to reserve judgement rather than to declare outrage when traditions appear to have been broken. Healthy growth is stimulated by constant evaluation and reassessment of all aspects in any subject. Now is a good time to be involved at whatever level in the unlimited horizons of studio ceramics if one keeps an open mind while acknowledging the validity of a wide range of approaches and interpretations without exclusions.

RECOMMENDED FURTHER READING

Billington, Dora: **The Technique of Pottery** (Batsford, London, 1966)

Birks, Tony: **The Art of the Modern Potter** (Country Life, London, 1970)

Cameron, Elizabeth and Lewis, Phillipa: **Potters on Pottery** (Evans, London, 1976)

Cardew, Michael: **Pioneer Pottery** (Longman, Harlow, Essex 1969; St. Martin's Press, New York, 1971)

Caiger-Smith, Alan: **Tin-glaze Pottery** (Faber & Faber, London, 1973)

Casson, Michael: **The Craft of the Potter** (BBC Publications, London, 1977)
Pottery in Britain Today (Tiranti, London, 1967)

Charleston, R.J. (Ed.): **World Ceramics** (Hamlyn, London, 1968)

Clark, Garth, and Hughto, Margie: **A Century of Ceramics in the United States 1878–1978** (E.P. Dutton, in association with the Everson Museum of Art, New York, 1979)

Clark, Garth: **American Potters** (Watson-Guptill, New York, 1981; Alphabooks, Sherborne)

Colson, Frank: **Kiln Building with Space-Age Materials** (**Van Nostrand, London & New York, 1975**)

Cooper, Emmanuel and Royle, Derek: **Glazes for the Studio Potter** (Batsford, London, 1978)

Cooper, Emmanuel: **A History of World Pottery** (Batsford, London, 1981)
Electric Kiln Pottery (Batsford, London, 1982)

Cowley, David: **Moulded and Slip-cast Pottery** (Batsford, London, 1978)

Dickerson, John: **Pottery Making: A Complete Guide** (Viking, New York, 1974)

Fournier, Robert: **Illustrated Dictionary of Practical Pottery** (Van Nostrand, London & New York, 1973)
Illustrated Dictionary of Pottery Form (Van Nostrand, London & New York, 1981)
David Leach: A Potter's Life with Workshop Notes (Fournier, Lacock, 1977)

Fraser, Harry: **Glazes for the Craft Potter** (Pitman, London, 1973 [now A & C Black]; Watson-Guptill, New York, 1974)

Green, David: **Understanding Pottery Glazes** (Faber & Faber, London, 1963)
A Handbook of Pottery Glazes (Faber & Faber, London, 1978)
Pottery: Materials and Techniques (Faber & Faber, London, 1967)

Hamer, Frank: **The Potter's Dictionary of Materials and Techniques** (Pitman, London, 1975 [now A & C Black]; Watson-Guptill, New York, 1975)

Hamilton, David: **Manual of Pottery and Ceramics** (Thames and Hudson, London, 1974)
Manual of Stoneware and Porcelain (Thames and Hudson, London, 1982)

Hettes and Rada: **Modern Ceramics** (Spring Books, London, 1965)

Holden, Andrew: **The Self-Reliant Potter** (A & C Black, London, 1982)

Honey, William: **The Art of the Potter** (Faber & Faber, London, 1946)

Hopper, Robin: **The Ceramic Spectrum:** A Simplified Approach to Glaze and Color Development (Chilton, Pennsylvania, 1983)

Houston, John (Ed.): **Lucie Rie** (Crafts Council, London, 1981)

Lane, Arthur: **Style in Pottery** (Faber & Faber, London, 1973)

Lane, Peter: **Studio Porcelain** (Pitman, London, 1980 [now A & C Black]; Chilton, Pennsylvania, 1980)

Leach, Bernard: **A Potter's Book** (Faber & Faber, London, 1945)
A Potter's Work (Adams and Dart, Bradford-on-Avon, Wilts., 1967)
The Potter's Challenge (Souvenir Press, London, 1976)

Lewenstein, Eileen, and Cooper, Emmanuel: **New Ceramics** (Studio Vista, London, 1974)

Mansfield, Janet (Ed.): **The Potter's Art: An Australian Collection** (Cassel, Australia)

Nelson, Glenn: **Ceramics** (Holt, Rhinehart & Winston, New York, 1966)

Parmalee, Cullen: **Ceramic Glazes** (Industrial Publications, Chicago, 1951)

Rhodes, Daniel: **Clay and Glazes for the Potter** (Chilton, Pennsylvania, 1973; Pitman, London, 1973)
Stoneware and Porcelain (Chilton, Pennsylvania, 1960; Pitman, London, 1960)
Pottery Form (Chilton, Pennsylvania, 1977; Pitman, London, 1978)

Rogers, Mary: **Pottery and Porcelain: A Handbuilder's Approach** (Alphabooks, Sherborne, 1979 [now Collins, London]; Watson-Guptill, New York, 1979)

Rose, Muriel: **Artist Potters in England** (Faber & Faber, London, 1970)

Shafer, Tom: **Pottery Decoration** (Watson-Guptill, New York, 1976; Pitman, London, 1976)

Wildenhain, Marguerite: **Pottery Form and Expression** (Van Nostrand Reinhold, New York, 1968)

Zakin, Richard: **Electric Kiln Ceramics** (Chilton, Pennsylvania, 1981)

Periodicals

American Craft (Published by the American Crafts Council, New York)
Ceramics Monthly, Ohio, USA
Ceramic Review, London (Published by The Craftsmen Potters' Association of Great Britain)
Crafts, London (Published by the Crafts Council)
New Zealand Potter, Wellington
Pottery in Australia (Published by the Potters' Society of Australia, Sydney)
Pottery Quarterly, Northfield Studio, Tring, Herts.
Studio Potter, New Hampshire, USA
Ceramica (Published by Antonio Vivas, Apartado 7008, Acacias 9, Madrid 5, Spain)

WHERE TO SEE STUDIO CERAMICS

Museums

The following list of museums and galleries is given as a guide to some of the places where permanent or occasional exhibitions of contemporary ceramics may be available.

AUSTRALIA

A.C.T.:	Australian National Gallery, Canberra
New South Wales:	Art Gallery of New South Wales, Sydney.
	Museum of Applied Arts and Sciences, Sydney.
	Newcastle Art Gallery, Newcastle
Northern Territory:	Art Gallery of the Northern Territory, Darwin
Queensland:	Art Gallery of Queensland, Brisbane
South Australia:	Art Gallery of South Australia, Adelaide
Tasmania:	Hobart Gallery and Museum, Hobart
Victoria:	National Gallery of Victoria, Melbourne.
	Victorian Ministry of the Arts, Melbourne
Western Australia:	Art Gallery of Western Australia, Perth

AUSTRIA

Vienna:	Österreiches Museum für Angewandte Kunst

BELGIUM

Brussels:	Koninklijk Museum voor Schone Kunsten
Gent:	Museum Hedendaagse Kunst en Museum voor Sierkunsten
Ostende:	Musée des Beaux Arts

CANADA

Nova Scotia:	Nova Scotia Museum, Halifax
Ontario:	Canada National Museum, Ottawa. Royal Ontario Museum, Toronto
Prince Edward Island:	The Confederation Centre Gallery and Museum, Charlottetown, Prince Edward Island
Quebec:	Montreal Museum of Fine Arts, Montreal.

CZECHOSLOVAKIA

Bechyne:	Museum of Contemporary Ceramics
Prague:	National Gallery. Museum of Decorative Arts

DENMARK

Copenhagen: Bing & Grondahl Factory
Museum
Kunstindustrimuseum.
The Royal Porcelain Manufactory

FRANCE

Marseilles: Musée Cantini, Marseilles
Paris: Musée des Arts Décoratifs
Villeneuve: Musée d'Art Moderne du Nord,
Allée du Musée, 59650
Villeneuve d'Ascq

GERMANY

Bremen: Bremer Landesmuseum für Kunst-
und Kulturgeschichte, Focke-
Museum, Schwachhauser
Heerstrasse, 2800 Bremen 1
Coburg: Kunstsammlungen der Veste
Coburg, Veste, 8630 Coburg
Deidesheim: Museum für moderne Keramik,
Stadtmauergasse 17, 6705
Deidesheim
Düsseldorf: Hetjens-Museum, Deutsches
Keramikmuseum, Palais
Nesselröde, Schulstrasse 4, 4000
Düsseldorf
Frankfurt: Museum für Kunsthandwerk,
Schaumainkai 15, 6000
Frankfurt 70
Frechen: Keramion, Museum für
zeitgenössische Keramische
Kunst, Bonnstrasse 12, 5020
Frechen
Hamburg: Museum für Kunst und Gewerbe,
Steintorplatz 1, 2000 Hamburg

Hannover: Kestner Museum, Trammplatz 3,
3000 Hannover
Höhr-Grenzhausen: Keramikmuseum Westerwald,
Historische und zeitgenössische
Keramik, Rathausstrasse 131,
5410 Höhr-Grenzhausen
Karlsruhe: Badisches Landesmuseum,
Schloss, 7500 Karlsruhe 1
Köln: Kunstgewerbemuseum der Stadt
Köln, Overstolzenhaus,
Rheingasse 8–12, 5000 Köln 1
Langerwehe: Topferei-Museum Langerwehe,
5163 Langerwehe
Leipzig: Museum des Kunsthandwerks
(Grassi-Museum),
Johannisplatz, DDR 7000
Leipzig
Ludwigshafen: Wilhelm-Hack-Museum, Berliner
Strasse 23, 6700 Ludwigshafen
München: Bayerisches Nationalmuseum,
Prinzregentenstrasse 3, 8000
München

Osnabrück: Kulturgeschichtliches Museum,
Heger-Tor-Wall, 4500
Osnabrück
Sögel: Emsland-Museum, Schloss
Clemenswerth, 4475 Sögel

HOLLAND

Amsterdam: Stedelijk Museum
Gröningen: Museum voor Stad en Lande
Rotterdam: Boymans van Beuningen Museum
The Hague: Gemeente Museum
Utrecht: Centraal Museum

ITALY

Faenza: Museo Internationale della
Ceramica

NEW ZEALAND

Auckland: National Museum
Christchurch: Wellington and McDougal
Gallery

NORWAY

Bergen: Vestlandske Kunstindustrimuseum
Oslo: Oslo Kunstindustrimuseum
Trondheim: Nordenfjeldkse
Kunstindustrimuseum

SWEDEN

Höganäs: Höganäs Museum
Stockholm: National Museum

SWITZERLAND

Geneva: Museum Ariane
Lausanne: Museum of Decorative Arts

UK

Aberdeen: Art Gallery and Museums,
Schoolhill, Aberdeen
Bath: Holbourne of Menstrie Museum,
Great Poulteney Street, Bath
Bedford: Cecil Higgins Art Gallery and
Museum, Castle Close, Bedford
Birmingham: Museum and Art Gallery,
Chamberlain Square,
Birmingham
Blackburn: Museum and Art Gallery, Library
Street, Blackburn
Bolton: Museum and Art Gallery, Le
Mans Crescent, Bolton
Bradford: Cartwright Hall Museum and Art
Gallery, Lister Park, Bradford
Brighton: Art Gallery and Museum, Church
Street, Brighton
Bristol: City Museum and Art Gallery,
Queens Road, Bristol
Cambridge: Fitzwilliam Museum,
Trumpington Street,
Cambridge
Cardiff: National Museum of Wales,
Cathays Park, Cardiff

Carlisle:	Museum and Art Gallery, Castle Street, Carlisle	Salford:	Museum and Art Gallery, Peel Park, The Crescent, Salford
Cheltenham:	Art Gallery and Museum, Clarence Street, Cheltenham	Sheffield:	City Museum, Weston Park, Sheffield
Colchester:	The Minories, 74 High Street, Colchester	Southampton:	City Museum and Art Gallery, Civic Centre, Southampton
Coventry:	Herbert Art Gallery and Museum, Jordan Well, Coventry	Stoke-on-Trent:	City Museum and Art Gallery, Broad Street, Hanley. Gladstone Pottery Museum, Uttoxeter Road, Longton
Derby:	Museum and Art Gallery, The Strand, Derby	Swansea:	Swansea Museum, Victoria Road, Swansea
Derbyshire:	Sudbury Hall, Sudbury	Tyne and Wear:	Shipley Art Gallery, Prince Consort Road, Gateshead. Sunderland Museum and Art Gallery, Borough Road, Sunderland
Edinburgh:	Huntley House Museum, 142 Canongate, Edinburgh. Royal Scottish Museum, Chambers Street, Edinburgh		
Exeter:	Royal Albert Memorial Museum, Queen Street, Exeter	York:	Castle Museum, York

USA

Glasgow:	Museum and Art Gallery, Kelvingrove, Glasgow
Gloucester:	City Museum and Art Gallery, Brunswick Road, Gloucester
Kendal:	Abbot Hall Art Gallery, Kendal, Cumbria
Hull:	Kingston-upon-Hull City Museum and Art Gallery, Queen Victoria Square, Hull. Ferens Art Gallery, Hull
Leeds:	City Art Gallery, Temple Newsam House, Leeds
Leicester:	Leicester Museum and Art Gallery, New Walk, Leicester
London:	Camden Arts Centre, Arkwright Road, NW3. Victoria and Albert Museum, Cromwell Road, SW7. Woodlands Art Gallery, 90 Mycenae Road, Blackheath, SE3
Manchester:	City Art Gallery, Mosley Street, Manchester. Whitworth Art Gallery, Whitworth Park, Manchester
Liverpool:	Liverpool Museum, William Brown Road, Liverpool
Newcastle-upon-Tyne:	Laing Art Gallery, Higham Place, Newcastle-upon-Tyne
Norwich:	Castle Museum, Castle Hill, Norwich. Sainsbury Centre for the Visual Arts, University of East Anglia, Norwich
Nottingham:	Castle Museum, The Castle, Nottingham
Oxford:	Ashmolean Museum, Beaumont Street, Oxford
Portsmouth:	City Museum and Art Gallery, Museum Road, Old Portsmouth
Reading:	Museum and Art Gallery, Blagrave Street, Reading

Arizona:	Phoenix Art Museum, 1625 North Central Ave., Phoenix
California:	Los Angeles County Museum, Los Angeles. Museum of Modern Art, San Francisco. Oakland Museum, Oakland
Colorado:	Denver Art Museum, Denver
Delaware:	Delaware Museum of Art
Indiana:	Indianapolis Museum of Art, 1200 West 28 Street
Michigan:	University of Michigan Art Museum
Missouri:	St. Louis Museum, St. Louis
New Jersey:	The Campbell Museum, Camden
New York:	American Craft Museum, 44 West 53 St, NYC. Everson Museum of Art, 401 Harrison St., Syracuse. Syracuse University, Syracuse. The Metropolitan Museum of Art, NYC. Whitney Museum of American Art, 945 Madison Ave., NYC
Oregon:	Portland Museum of Art, Portland
Pennsylvania:	Philadelphia Museum of Art, Philadelphia
Texas:	Witte Museum, San Antonio
Utah:	Utah Museum of Fine Arts, Salt Lake City
Washington:	Seattle Art Museum, Seattle
Washington D.C.	Renwick Gallery, National Museum of American Art, Smithsonian Institution, Washington D.C.
Wisconsin:	John Michael Kohler Arts Center, Sheboygan

Galleries

AUSTRALIA

A.C.T.:
Beaver Galleries, 9 Investigator Street, Red Hill 2603
Solander Gallery, 2 Solander Court, Yarralumla 2600

New South Wales:
Aladdin Gallery, 45 Elizabeth Bay Road, Sydney
Australian Craftworks, The Old Police Station, 127 George Street, Sydney
The Australian Design Centre, 70 George Street, The Rocks, Sydney 2000
Blackfriars Gallery, 172 St Johns Road, Glebe
Inner City Clayworkers Gallery, 103 St Johns Road, Glebe 2037
Laburnum Gallery, 9a Salisbury Avenue, Blackburn, NSW 3130
Manly Art Gallery, West Esplanade, Manly 2095
Market Row Gallery, 228 Clarence Street, Sydney 2000
Old Bakery Gallery, 22 Rosenthal Avenue, Lane Cove
The Potters' Gallery, 48 Burton Street, Darlinghurst, Sydney
Seasons Gallery, Range Road, North Sydney 2060

Queensland:
Australian Craft, 2 Waitomo Plaza, Cnr. Davonport & Hicks Sts., Southport 4215
Joy Bowman Galleries, 6 Leichhardt Street, Spring Hill 4000
Vintu Gallery, 57 MacGregor Terrace, Bardon 4065

South Australia:
Elmswood Fine Craft, 312 Unley Road, Hyde Park, Adelaide
Festival Centre Gallery, Adelaide
The Jam Factory Craft Centre, 169 Payneham Road, St Peters, Stepney

Tasmania:
Aspect Design, 79 Salamanca Place, Hobart 7000
Handmark Gallery, 44–6 Hampden Road, Battery Point, Hobart 7000

Victoria:
Ceramics Gallery, No 107 The Jam Factory, Chapel Street, South Yarra 3141
Distelfink Gallery, 432 Burwood Road, Hawthorne 3122
Meat Market Craft Centre, Melbourne
Walker Ceramics Gallery, 826 Glenferrie Road, Hawthorn

Western Australia:
Joan Campbell Potters Workshop, Fremantle
Tenmoku Gallery, Napoleon Close, Cottisloe

CANADA

Alberta:
Quest Gallery, 105 Banff Avenue, Banff

British Columbia:
Quest Gallery, 1023 Government Street, Victoria

GERMANY

Berlin:
Kunst und handwerk, Fasanenstrasse 11, 1000 Berlin 12

Darmstadt:
Galerie Charlotte Hennig, Rheinstrasse 18, 6100 Darmstadt.
Kunsthandwerk + Galerie Terra, Hedelberger Strasse 104, 6100 Darmstadt

Essen:
Bredeneyer Galerie, Bredeneyer Strasse 19, 4300 Essen 1

Freiburg-Günterstal:
Keramik-Galerie, Dr. G + E Schneider, Reidbergstrasse 33, 7800 Freiburg-Günterstal

Hamburg:
Galerie der Kunsthandwerker, Danziger Strasse 40, 2000 Hamburg.
Galerie L, Heine-Haus, Elbchausee 31, 2000 Hamburg

Hannover:
Keramik-Galerie Böwig, Am Ballhof-Kreuzstrasse 1, 3000 Hannover

Heidelberg:
Galerie Somers, Ladenburger Strasse 21, 6900 Heidelberg

Heilbron:
Galerie Keramika, Ursula Felzman, Am Wollhaus 18, 7100 Heilbron

Kiel:
Galerie Terrakotta, Feldstrasse 40, 2300 Kiel

Koblenz:
Galerie Handwerk, Rizzastrasse 24–26, 5400 Koblenz

Köln:
Galerie An Gross St. Martin, An Gross St. Martin Nr. 6, 5000 Köln 1

Mönchen Gladbach:
Kunstkammer Dr. Köster, Albertusstrasse 4, 4050 Mönchen Gladbach

München:
Galerie Handwerk, Handwerkspflege in Bayern, Ottostrasse 7, 8000 München

Oberhausen:
Keramik-Studio Edith Sommerfeld, Grenzstrasse 33, 4200 Oberhausen

Osnabrück:
Keramik-Galerie Wulfter Turm, Sutthauser Strasse 354, 5400 Osnabrück

Nürnberg:
Prager Galerie, Albrecht-Dürer-Strasse 30–35, 8500 Nürnberg

Sögel: Forum Form Clemenswerth, Schloss Clemenswerth, 4475 Sögel

Stuttgart: Potter's Gallery, Calwer Strasse 56, 7000 Stuttgart

Syke: Galerie Dr. Fritz Vehring, Bremer Weg 4, 2800 Syke

Weisbaden: Keramik-Studio Helga Thurow, An den Quellen 4, 6200 Weisbaden

NEW ZEALAND

Auckland: Auckland City Art Gallery, Wellesley Street

Christchurch: Robert McDougall Art Gallery, Botanical Gardens

Dunedin: Dunedin Public Art Gallery, Logan Park

Hamilton: Waikato Art Museum, Investment House, London Street

Masterton: Wairarapa Arts Centre, Bruce Street

Napier: Hawke's Bay Art Gallery and Museum, Herschell Street

New Plymouth: Govett-Brewster Art Gallery, Queen Street, off Devon Street

Palmerston North: Manawatu Art Gallery, 398 Main Street

Wanganui: Sarjeant Art Gallery, Queens Park

Wellington: Dowse Art Gallery, Laings Road, Lower Hutt
National Art Gallery, Museum Building, Buckle Street

NORWAY

Bryne: Galleri Vaaland, Bryne

Moss: Tendenser Galleri F15, Jelöya, Moss

Oslo: Galleri U-2, Oslo

UK

Banbury: Prestcote Gallery, Cropredy, Banbury

Bath: Beaux Arts, York Street, Bath

Brighton: Barclaycraft, 7 East Street, Brighton

Cambridge: Primavera, 10 King's Parade, Cambridge

Chester: Three King's Studios, Lower Bridge Street, Chester

Chichester: Hands Craft Gallery, 150 St. Pancras, Chichester

Cornwall: New Craftsman, 24 Fore Street, St. Ives

Coventry: Centre Crafts, 169 Spon Street, Coventry

Cumbria: Corn Mill Galleries, The Old Town Mill, Ulverston

Derbyshire: Yew Tree Gallery, The Square, Ellastone

Devon: Dartington Craft Shop and Cider Press Gallery, Shinner's Bridge, Dartington.
Palace Gate Gallery, 1 Deanery Place, Palace Gate, Exeter.
Windjammer Crafts Gallery, Russell Court, Fore Street, Salcombe

Edinburgh: The Scottish Craft Centre, 140 Canongate, Royal Mile, Edinburgh

Gloucestershire: Chestnut Gallery, High Street, Bourton-on-the-Water

Herefordshire: Collection Craft Gallery, 13 Southend, Ledbury

Lancashire: Wolf House Gallery, Nr. Jenny Brown's Point, Gibralter, Silverdale, Carnforth

Leeds: Craft Centre and Design Gallery, City Art Gallery, The Headrow, Leeds

Lincoln: Regional Craft Centre, Jews Court, Steep Hill, Lincoln

Liverpool: Bluecoat Display Centre, Bluecoat Chambers, School Lane, Liverpool

London: Amalgam, 3 Barnes High Street, SW3. Aspects, 3–5 Whitfield Street, W1.
British Crafts Centre, 43 Earlham Street, Covent Garden, WC2.
Casson Gallery, 73 Marylebone High Street, W1.
Christopher Wood Gallery, 15 Motcomb Street, Belgravia, SW1.
Crafts Council Gallery, 12 Waterloo Place, SW1.
Craftshop, Victoria and Albert Museum, Cromwell Road, SW7.
Craftsmen Potters' Shop, William Blake House, Marshall Street, W1.
Innate Harmony, 67 St. John's Wood High Street, NW8.
Dan Klein, 11 Halkin Arcade, Motcomb Street, Belgravia, SW1.
David Mellor, 26 St. James Street, WC1.
Paul Rice, 60 Blenheim Crescent, W11

Manchester: Royal Exchange Theatre Craft Centre, St. Ann's Square, Manchester

Northhampton:	Four Seasons Gallery, 39 St. Giles Street, Northampton	Michigan:	Carol Hooberman Gallery, 155 South Bates, Birmingham
Norwich:	Black Horse Craft Centre, 10b Wensum Street, Norwich.	Missouri:	Craft Alliance, 6640 Delmer Boulevard, St. Louis
	Castle Museum Craft Shop and Index, Norwich Castle	New York:	Atlantic Gallery, 458 W. Broadway, NYC.
Nottingham:	Focus Gallery, 108 Derby Road, Nottingham		Elements Gallery, 766 Madison Avenue, NYC.
Oxford:	Oxford Gallery, 23 High Street, Oxford		Greenwich House Gallery, 16 Jones Street, NYC.
Southampton:	Southampton Art Gallery, Civic Centre, Commercial Road, Southampton		Hadler/Rodriguez Gallery, 38 East 57 Street, NYC.
Suffolk:	Aldringham Craft Market, Nr. Leiston.		Hopper's Gallery, 647 South Avenue, NYC.
	Falcon House Gallery, Swan Street, Boxford		Incorporated Gallery, 1200 Madison Avenue, NYC.
Sussex:	The Craftsman, 8 High Street, Ditchling		The Porcelain Crafts Studio, 74 Fifth Avenue, NYC.
Warwickshire:	Peter Dingley Gallery, 16 Meer Street, Stratford-upon-Avon	Pennsylvania:	Clay Studio Gallery, 49 North Second Street, Philadelphia.
Wiltshire:	Katherine House Gallery, The Parade, Marlborough		Helen Drutt Gallery, Philadelphia.
			Nexus Gallery, 2017 Chancellor Street, Philadelphia
USA		Washington:	Fireworks Gallery, Grand Central Arcade, 214 1st Avenue South, Seattle
Arizona:	The Hand and the Spirit Gallery, 4222 North Marshall Way, Scottsdale.	Washington D.C.	Branch Gallery, 1063 Wisconsin Avenue, Northwest, Washington
	The Mind's Eye, 4200 North Marshall Way, Scottsdale	West Virginia:	Huntington Galleries, Park Hills, Huntington
California:	Louis Newman Galleries, 322 N. Beverly Drive, Beverly Hills.		
	Garth Clark Gallery, 5280 Wiltshire Boulevard, Los Angeles.		
	Elizabeth Fortner Gallery, 1114 State Street, Santa Barbara.		
	The Quay Gallery, 254 Sutter Street, San Francisco.		
	Marcia Rodell Gallery, 11714 San Vincente Boulevard, San Vincente		
Florida:	Image of Sarasota Gallery, Sarasota		
Illinois:	Exhibit A, 233 E. Ontario Street, Chicago		
Kentucky:	Images, 1835 Hampden Court, Louisville		
Massachusetts:	Impressions Gallery, 275 Dartmouth Street, Boston.		
	The Society of Arts and Crafts, 175 Newbury Street, Boston.		
	Westminster Gallery, 132a Newbury Street, Boston.		
	Ten Arrow Gallery, 10 Arrow Street, Cambridge.		
	Stebbins Gallery, Church Street, Cambridge		

INDEX

Page numbers in **bold type** refer to captions and illustrations.